CONTENTS.

	PAGE
INTRODUCTION,	5

CHAPTER I.—SOMNAMBULISM AND PSYCHIC PHENOMENA, ... 9

    The Hypnotic, Mesmeric, and the Psychic States. Hypnotism a Curative Agent; the Sixth Sense; Dreams, Premonitions; Double and Psychic Consciousness. Evidences of the Soul within us.

CHAPTER II.—CLAIRVOYANCE, ... 23

    Psychoscopy, or Soul Sight. Spiritual Faculty, exhibited by religious ecstatics, not a common possession. How Cultivated. The Opinions and Evidence of Men of Science. Second Sight. The Utility of Soul-Sight.

CHAPTER III.—CLAIRVOYANCE ILLUSTRATED, ... 33

    Classified. Strange Story of the Chicago Water Supply. Lost Goods Restored. An Aid to the Physician. Experiments in Rothesay. Remarkable Clairvoyants. Clairvoyance in Mesmerism and in Spiritualism.

CHAPTER IV.—PSYCHOMETRY, ... 53

    Soul-Measuring and Soul-Measurers. Dr. Buchanan's Discoveries. Professor Denton's Experiments. Detective's Clues; what Psychometry can do. Testimony of Mr. Stead and the Rev. Minot J. Savage. Disease Detected, and Character Gauged by this Faculty.

CHAPTER V.—THOUGHT-TRANSFERENCE AND 69

Telepathy,

Explained and Defined. Transference of Taste in Mesmerism. Thought-Transference, in Dreams, from the Dying to the Living; the Dead to the Living; in Prayer; in ordinary Experience. Incidents and Experiences, etc. Mark Twain, Hudson Tuttle, and Dr. Hilden.

Chapter VI.—Thought-Reading Experiments, 88

Thought and Muscle-Reading Distinguished. Projecting Mental Pictures. Normal Experiments, without contact, by Professor Lodge, Mr. Guthrie, and Professor Barrett. Some Practical Suggestions. Muscle-Reading Entertainments. Directions.

Chapter VII.—Spiritualism, 102

"How to Thought-Read" and Phenomenal Spiritualism. The Spirit within us. The rejection of the Psychic. The Fraudulent in Spiritualism. Spiritualism without Spirits. Thought-Reading by Spirits and Mediums.

Chapter VIII.—Spiritualism.—*Continued*, 115

Automatic Writing. A Test Medium. Trance Addresses. A Direct Spirit-Painting. Reflections and Speculations. Testimony of Cromwell F. Varley, F.R.S., the Electrician. Theosophy a Revised Version of Hindoo Metempsychosis, etc. etc.

INTRODUCTION.

THE first book of this series, "How to Mesmerise," gave so much satisfaction to the reading public, and having passed into several editions, my publishers have asked me to write another work on similar lines. This *brochure* is my response. Clairvoyance, Psychometry, and Thought Transference—briefly referred to in the former—are more fully gone into in this. Consequently, I have little doubt "How to Thought-Read" will meet with acceptance.

Thought-reading is duly considered and explained. A clear distinction is drawn between Musculation, or Muscle and Mind-Reading; and although these pages are not confined to Thought-Reading, as generally understood by the public, the subject itself, and as an entertainment, have been pretty fully dealt with.

During the past decade, psychological subjects have, in a remarkable way, arrested public attention. "New Mesmerism" and "New Spiritualism" are popular subjects with editors and magazine writers. Whatever the real causes—a greater influx of the spiritual from "the state of the dead," or from a reaction in the minds of men against the purblind materialism of our scientific leaders—it is hard to say. Possibly these and other causes have been at work. One thing is certain, for good or ill, the majority of thinking men and women of the age are not only interested in, but are actually searching for evidence of "embodied spirit." Hence we find men of science, journalists, and even professed materialists and secularists, who, a few years ago, could scarcely speak of these subjects in the ordinary language of courtesy, confess now not only their belief, but are going to the other extreme of advocating, what as yet, they have failed to fully grasp.

A few years ago "The British Parliament of Science" was nothing if not materialistic. The leading *savants* of the day declared "all was matter, no matter what." Consequently, man was the highest product of protoplasm, and his *only* destiny the grave. The change has been great indeed, when one of its most brilliant members (Professor Oliver Lodge, D.Sc., F.R.S., British Association at Cardiff, 1891) in his address said: "It is familiar that a thought may be excited on the brain of another person, transferred thither from our brain by pulling a suitable trigger; by liberating energy in the form of sound, for instance, or by the mechanical act of writing, or in other ways. A pre-arranged code, called language, and a material medium of communication, are recognised methods. May there not, also, be an *immaterial* (perhaps an ethereal) medium of communication? Is it possible that an idea can be transferred from one person to another by a process such as we have not yet grown accustomed to, and know practically nothing about? *In this case I have evidence. I assert I have seen it done, and am perfectly convinced of the fact; many others are satisfied of the truth, too.* It is, perhaps, a natural consequence of the community of life or family relationship running through all living beings. The transmission of life may be likened in some ways to the transmission of magnetism, and all magnets are sympathetically connected, so that, if suitably suspended, a vibration from one disturbs others, even though they be distant 92,000,000 miles. It is sometimes objected that, granting thought-transference or telepathy to be a fact, it belongs more especially to lower forms of life, and that as the cerebral hemispheres develop we become independent of it; that what we notice is the relic of a decaying faculty, not the germ of a new and fruitful sense, and that progress is not to be made by studying or alluding to it. As well might the objection be urged against a study of embryology. *It may, on the other hand, be an indication of a higher mode of communication, which shall survive our temporary connection with ordinary matter.* The whole region is unexplored territory, and it is conceivable that matter may react on mind in a way we can at present only dimly imagine." The italics are mine.

Thought-Transference and Telepathy may, indeed, be an indication of a higher mode of communication between human beings after we have severed our temporary connection with matter. Whether or not, the hope should repay our study. I have sought in the following pages to briefly define and illustrate what these phases of communication are.

Double and Psychic Consciousness, Clairvoyance, natural and induced; Psychometry, its natural and leading features as a spiritual faculty; Thought-Transference, visions, dreams, and their *portents*, are in turn briefly dealt with, in order to extract therefrom some evidence of *soul*.

Modern Spiritualism is referred to, in so far as Thought-Reading is likely to throw any light upon its psychological phases, as well as on its physical phenomena.

While attempting to cover so much ground my difficulty was not what to write, but what not to write, the materials at my disposal being so abundant. Much has been cut down to get the whole within reasonable compass. Nevertheless, I hope my readers will find "How to Thought-Read" a readable contribution to the science of soul.

JAMES COATES.

GLENBEG,
ARDBEG, ROTHESAY, N. B.

EXPERIMENT IN PSYCHOMETRY.—See Page 60.

MR. and MRS. COATES.

CHAPTER I.

SOMNAMBULISM AND PSYCHIC PHENOMENA.

BEFORE entering upon the subject of "How to Thought Read"—or rather, range of interesting subjects grouped under this title—it is proposed to deal briefly with the key to the whole, which is to be found in the revelations of man's inner life, soul-life and character, presented by somnambulism and trance, whether natural or induced.

The use of a few simple terms having a well-defined meaning will help the reader and prepare him for the more careful study of the psychic side of human life.

The somnambulistic and trance states may be divided, for the convenience of examination, into the Hypnotic, or state of hypnosis; the Mesmeric, or somnambulistic; and the Psychic, or lucid somnambulistic—or briefly, the Hypnotic, Mesmeric, and Psychic states.

The operator is the controlling agent, hypnotist, or mesmerist; in spiritualism, the guide or control.

The sensitive is the subject, the percipient, psychic, patient, or person who passes into the hypnotic, mesmeric, or trance states, etc.

Hypnosis is the term used for the hypnotic state artificially induced by the agent. Hypnosis is the lowest rung of the ladder; the psychic or soul state the highest. The intermediate phases, as indicated in conscious or sub-conscious conditions of life, are innumerable and not readily classified. Still, the states mentioned will give a favourable insight to the whole. In hypnosis, physical rather than mental phenomena are evolved; *anæsthesia*, or non-sensitiveness to pain, is more or less present. The senses of smell and hearing are partially exalted, and the sensitive may be partially or wholly unconscious.

The mesmeric state is the term frequently used to denote ordinary artificial somnambulism. It is actually the higher or more perfect form of hypnosis. The senses in this state are more fully submerged, and the mental faculties are more fully exalted, than in hypnosis.

The psychic state, as the mesmeric, relates to the mental, and hypnosis to the more physical, so does the psychic state refer to that class of extraordinary somnambulism in which the mental and the spiritual gifts transcend in character and power those of the foregoing states. In this state the higher phenomena of lucid somnambulism, clairvoyance, and thought-transference are manifested more perfectly than in any other.

The hypnotic, the mesmeric, and the psychic states indicated are frequently interlinked in manifestation. The sensitive may pass from the first to the last without apparent gradation. It is well to keep these divisions in thought, so that in practice no one will be content with the *lower* where it is possible, by wise and judicious observations and operations, to induce the higher.

To make the matter still more clear, in hypnosis and in the mesmeric state all phenomena may be said to be induced through and by the influence and the direction of the operator. Not that he produces the effects as they are exhibited by the sensitive, but they are brought about through the agency of his suggestions or operations.

In the psychic state this is not always the case. The influence of the operator may at times be almost *nil*. The operator will find it best—when the sensitive is in a high lucid state—to become an observer and a learner, and no longer continue the *rôle* of director.

In the psychic state, the soul-powers, so often submerged in ordinary life, transcend in a remarkable manner. The senses are completely suspended and the mind exalted to such a degree, a clearly defined super-sensuous condition is reached. Whether this stage or condition is induced by fasting, prayer, disease, or by mesmeric agencies, matters little. In it we find the key to the seership, and the clairvoyance, and the prophetic utterance, and the mystic powers attributed to and exercised by prophet, and seer, and sybil in the past. By the investigation of the phenomena evolved by the psychic state we are enabled to understand something of man's soul or spiritual nature, apart from the phenomena induced by pathological conditions of brain and body.

The foregoing view presented of mesmeric conditions may be very different from that which medical men may glean from hypnotic practice with hysterical and lobsided patients, and certainly not the views which the general public are likely to gather from seeing a number of paid "subjects" knocked about a music hall stage by an ignorant showman.

From the roughest to the finest, from matter to spirit, from hypnosis to the psychic state, we find enough to arrest attention and give a high degree of seriousness and earnestness to our investigation. We stand on the threshold of soul, and the place where we stand is holy ground. We find, as is the physical, mental, and spiritual characteristics of the operator, *plus* those of the sensitive or sensitives, so will be the nature of the phenomena evolved.

It will be observed some subjects never get beyond the first state, or hypnosis; others that of the second, or mesmeric. All sensitives, in keeping with their temperamental and mental developments (as revealed by phrenology and psychometry), are better adapted for one class of phenomena than that of others.

It may be further observed that the foregoing states may be self-induced or, directly and indirectly, the product of "spirit-control," drugs, or bodily disease. Hypnosis, we must bear in mind, although not unlike the mesmeric state, has no more relation to that condition than sleep produced by an exhaustive walk or a dose of laudanum is like natural or healthy sleep. Indeed, hypnosis is not properly a condition of sleep. In the majority of cases the sensitive is never wholly unconscious. It is rather a state in which there is a temporary perversion or subordination between brain impressions and consciousness. The sensitive in hypnosis is often less intelligent than in the normal or waking state.

For various reasons the state of hypnosis may be recognised as that state in which the mind is subjected to certain abnormal conditions of the body, notably of the brain, spinal cord, and indirectly of the circulation, induced by certain means determined upon by the operator. The mental condition in this state is one of almost pure automatism, in which hallucination or sense illusions are more or less present.

Great and serious are the responsibilities of those who bring about the state of hypnosis. Every thought and feeling, of whatever kind, infused in this state, like seed, will take root and germinate, and finally bud into action in the daily or waking consciousness, and determine unconsciously for the sensitive the character of his life. Hypnotism is neither for indiscriminate use, nor is hypnosis to be induced as a plaything for the thoughtless—medical or lay. At the same time, in the hands of the thoughtful, its educative value is most important, for, if the operator is well poised, and feels that, he can impart higher thoughts and strengthen the will[A] of the sensitives by the twofold agencies of impressionability and suggestion. This is something not to be despised. It is surely no degradation to be saved from evils one cannot overcome or resist, unless assisted by external aid, even though that help can only come by submitting to hypnotism.

In hypnosis the outer brain of convoluted grey matter is most affected, being more or less denuded of arterial and nervous stimuli. The power of conscious, intellectual, and abstract thought is reduced to a minimum. The organs of the central brain are differently influenced, as in inverse ratio the stimulation is increased. The eye is more susceptible to light, or the pupils may become dilated and fixed. The auditory sense is rendered more keen. The olfactory powers are intensified, and there is more or less insensibility of feeling. The powers of co-ordination and locomotion are preserved up to a certain stage, when these functions are disturbed, all power of voluntary movement ceases, lethargic and cataleptic symptoms supervene.

It was by observing, more particularly, hypnosis, Professor Heidenhain was led to aver "inhibition" actually accounted for all phases of hypnotism. This opinion has evidently been based on a limited number of cases. "No inhibition," says Dr. Drayton, "however ingeniously applied, will explain all the phenomena of magnetism. If the personal consciousness, the individuality, of the subject has been lost, and his state is that of automatism, or rather that of an involuntary actor, certainly his cerebral functions operate in a manner entirely distinct from that which is characteristic in his ordinary state. The inhibition relates to his common order of conduct mentally, while the super-sensitivity and extraordinary play of faculty that he may exhibit, indicate a higher phase of sensory activity, more free or harmonious co-ordination of the cerebral functions. The brakes are off, hence the phenomena that are frequently observed in the somnambulist, and awaken wonder, because so much out of keeping with what is known of his common life."

Here we find doctors—experts in hypnotism or mesmerism—agree to differ. They agree in this, albeit not expressly stated, they are alike positive and decided in their views, and certainly *without being positive, there is no possible success as an operator.*

The mistake they make evidently arises in confounding the two states (hypnosis and the mesmeric), one with the other. There is no super-sensitivity, or extraordinary play of faculty in hypnosis, whatever there may be in the mesmeric state. They are similar, in that they may be both induced by the reduction of the activity of the cerebral cortex.

In hypnosis the mind slumbers and dreams. The dream-life appears as substantial to the sensitive as the waking life. The life creations, thus dreamed of, are acted upon, whether they arise from suggestion or other causes.

In the mesmeric state the senses slumber, and the mind awakens to a fuller enfranchisement of existence, and to the exhibition of mental and spiritual powers not hitherto suspected.

In the lower stages the increased power of the senses is to be found in the *intense concentration* of effort, brought about from the fact that the subject's attention is, and his whole energies are, directed in one line of action or thought, to the exclusion of mind or brain activity in other directions. Hence all efforts are centred in the direction suggested by the operator, or self-induced, as suggested by the "dominant idea."

The sensitive exhibits powers of mind and ability of thought which were not noticeable in the ordinary waking condition. Not because he really possesses greater powers of mind or body, but because of the lack of concentration in the waking state. By this concentration of direction, so called abnormal feats of strength are performed, rigidity of structure brought about, and other characteristics not peculiar to common life. In a higher sense, we see the sensitive passing from this condition of concentration of one-idea-ism to a spiritual state, in which the phenomena exhibited are no longer the product of self-dethronement and of suggestion. Higher still, we see the soul reign supreme. The sensitive possesses a clear consciousness of what is transpiring at home and abroad, according to the direction of his psychic powers.

In the psychic state—the more perfect trance state or control—the whole mind becomes illumined; past, present, and future become presentable to the mind of the lucid somnambulist as one great whole. This higher stage may be reached through the simple processes of manipulation, and passes as suggested in my little work, "How to Mesmerise."

In the mesmeric state the sensitive passes from the mere automatism of the earlier stages of hypnosis to the distinct individuality indicated above, although still more or less influenced or directed by his controller or operator into the line of thought and train of actions most desired.

The difference between the hypnotic and mesmeric states should now be very clear. In the former the sensitive has no identity, in the latter his identity is preserved in a clearly individualised form throughout the whole series of abnormal acts. Whenever the sensitive enters this condition his personal consciousness is most apparent in the middle and higher stages.

In fact, in the mesmeric state, it is very stupid for some operators to ask the sensitive, "Are you asleep?" It may be understood what is meant, yet the question is absurd from the standpoint of an intelligent observer. The sensitive is never more awake. The higher the state the greater the wakefulness and lucidity of the inner or soul life.

THE SIXTH SENSE.

In the mesmeric state we see developed what Lord Kelvin (Professor Thomson, of Glasgow University), Drs. Baird, Hammond, and Drayton call the magnetic sense—or "sixth sense." It is a gift of super-sensitiveness. To my mind it is something more, the enfranchisement of the soul, the human ego—in proportion as the dominance of the senses is arrested.

In blindness, it has been noticed how keen the sense of touch becomes. I have also noticed the keen sensitiveness of facial perception enjoyed by some of the blind, by which they are enabled to perceive objects in the absence of physical sight. In the mesmeric state we see a somewhat analogous mental condition. As the peculiar sense of the blind is developed by extra concentration of the mind in the direction of facial perception, so is "the sixth sense" developed by concentration of direction, as well as by the condition of sensitiveness induced by the mesmeric state.

This newly recognised sense, "the sixth sense," not only answers the purpose of sight and hearing, but transcends all senses in vividness and power. Materialists, no longer able to ignore the phenomena of somnambulism and trance, and compelled to admit man's avenues of knowledge in this life were not confined to the recognised five senses, are good enough to give him a "sixth sense," even while they deny him a soul. In the same way, no longer able to deny the existence of mesmerism, they now admit it to consideration—re-baptised as hypnotism. The phenomena being admitted, we will not quarrel over the names by which they are called.

PSYCHIC-CONSCIOUSNESS.

As we advance in our investigations we find in the higher conditions of these states a double or treble consciousness or memory. The higher including and overlapping the lower. Thus the consciousness of the hypnotic state includes that of the waking state, while the memory of the waking state possesses no conscious recollection of what has taken place in hypnosis, and so on, each stage has its own phases of consciousness. The memory of the sensitive, under influence, overlapping and including the memory of ordinary or normal life.

Strange as it may appear, there are no phenomena which have been evolved in any of these abnormal conditions of life, which have not been observed again and again in ordinary or normal life, as well authenticated instances of dreams, warnings, and telepathy testify.

Dr. Richardson notwithstanding, "in dreams and visions of the night" God has manifested himself to man in all ages. In other words, the soul (in sleep and analogous states to somnambulism and trance) comes more in touch with the sub-conscious or soul sphere of thought and existence. At times there is an inrush from that sphere into our present conscious state, by which we know of things which could not otherwise be known. Of dreams, our space will not admit more than occasional reference, we may mention as a case in point the dream of Mrs. Donan, wife of the livery stableman from whom Dr. Cronin hired his horse in Chicago. A week before Dr. Cronin was murdered this lady had a dream-vision, and dreamt he was barbarously murdered, and saw in a vision the whole terrible scene. This dream was a means, first, of forewarning the doctor, and second, of leading to the detection of the miscreants.

Of premonitions, an incident reported in the *Register* of Adelaide, will suffice:—"Constable J. C. H. Williams has reported to headquarters that he had an unpleasant experience at about midnight on Monday. He was on duty at the government offices in King William Street, and while standing at the main entrance he had a presentiment that he was in danger, and walked away a few steps. Scarcely had he moved from the spot, when a portion of the cornice work at the top of the building fell with a crash on the place where he had been standing. The piece of plaster must have weighed fully a stone, and had it struck Williams the result would doubtless have been fatal. A passer-by saw the constable a few minutes after, and his scared looks and agitated manner clearly showed that his story was true." Concerning telepathy, Mrs. Andrew Crosse, the distinguished widow of the famous electrician, relates in *Temple Bar* an anecdote about the late Bishop Wilberforce, to the effect, the Bishop was writing a dry business letter one day, when a feeling of acute mental agony overcame him and he felt that some evil had befallen his favourite son, a midshipman in the navy. The impression was correct. On that very day the lad, who was with his ship in the Pacific, had been wounded and nearly bled to death. When this was told Hallam, the historian, he replied that a very similar thing had happened to himself. A few cases are noted further on. Some persons would repudiate *all* such incidents as accidents or coincidences; while others would fly to the extreme, and declare all such are the result of "spirit control"—that is, some disembodied but friendly spirit projected the dream, conveyed the warning, or telepathically despatched the news. But we must never forget news has to be received as well as despatched. Consequently, we, as embodied spirits, must possess psychic consciousness.

I believe that *much* of the phenomena, directly and indirectly attributed to disincarnate spirit control, are traceable to *no other source* than the powers of our own embodied spirits, as revealed by the facts of somnambulism and trance, and this is the opinion of all intelligent spiritualists.

"Because," says Mr. G. H. Stebbins, a prominent investigator of modern spiritualism in the United States "a person quotes from books he never saw, or *tells of what he never knew* in any external way, that is not final proof that he is under an external spirit control. Psychometry and clairvoyance may sometimes solve it all."

"I hold," says Mr. Myers, "that telepathy and clairvoyance do, in fact, exist—telepathy, a communication between incarnate mind and incarnate mind, and perhaps between incarnate minds and minds unembodied; clairvoyance, a knowledge of things terrene which over-passes the limits of ordinary perception, and which, perhaps, achieves an insight with some other than terrene world."

These are the cautious admissions of eminent investigators in psychical research.

DOUBLE OR SUB-CONSCIOUSNESS.

"There are two sets," says Dr. Brown-Sequard, "a double state of mental powers in the human organism, essentially differing from each other. The one may be designated as ordinary conscious intelligence; the other, a superior power, which controls our better nature."

J. Balfour Brown, in his "Medical Jurisprudence," says:—"In no case of pure somnambulism, waking consciousness of the individual knows anything of the sleeping consciousness. It is as if there were two distinct memories."

This double-consciousness, memory, or sub-state of mental powers, is another but lower phase of psychic-consciousness, and is sometimes exhibited by accidents, and also by disease.

Dr. Abercromby relates the case of a boy, four years old who was trepanned for a fracture of the skull. He was in a *complete stupor* during the operation, and was not conscious of what took place. At fifteen he became seriously ill of fever. In the delirium occasioned by the fever, he gave a correct description of the operation, *and of all the persons present, their dress*, manners, and actions, to the minutest particulars. The "superior power" must have obtained this knowledge in some other way than through the ordinary channels of the outward senses.

In cases of apparent drowning, where the person has been saved from death by active, external help, we have been informed that the human mind has worked with a rapidity of action not thought possible in the waking state, the intensity of menial action being increased in adverse ratio to the inaction of the external senses and consciousness. In this state the career of a lifetime has been reviewed, conversations, actions, persons seen and places visited, all vividly brought to mind—in possibly less time than it takes to pen this paragraph. These phenomena suggest the reflection that the daily waking life—sensuous and worldly-minded—is possibly, to many, the least real and effective. How much our external life is influenced by our unconscious (to us in the waking state) sub-life, is an interesting problem.

Dr. Oliver Wendell Holmes says:—"The more we examine the mechanism of thought, the more we shall see that the automatic and unconscious action of the mind enters largely into all its processes. We *all* have a *double* who is wiser and better than we, who puts thoughts into our heads and words into our mouths."

A commercial gentleman of my acquaintance, who was rather sceptical on the subject of double-consciousness—although, "notwithstanding," he said, "Mr. Stead, in the *Review of Reviews*, had turned an honest penny out of ghosts, double-consciousness, and that sort of rubbish"—admitted to me, he had a maid, who had an awkward habit of rising in her sleep, carefully setting the fires, cleaning and dusting out the rooms, setting the breakfast table, and doing many other things which appeared important to the servant-mind. Her movements were watched. She slipped about with eyes closed, avoiding obstacles, and doing her work systematically and neatly, and without fuss, when done, she would go to bed. In the morning she had no recollection of what she had said or done. It was a curious thing, he had to admit. The girl was honest enough. He was certain this habit had not been simulated. Threats of discharge, and possible loss of wages, did not cure her of this habit. There was a certain form of "double consciousness" in this case.

"The subliminal consciousness" of Mr. Myers, by which he accounts for the phenomena of genius, is but another way of expressing the concept of an "identity underlying all consciousness," the psyche, the real "I, me," "the superior power which directs and controls our better nature," the "double who is wiser and better than we," the reality of which is so much hidden from our ordinary experience, because our soul-life is so much buried out of sight by the *débris* of the "things of this life," which, fortunately or otherwise, pre-occupy so much of our attention.

It is this "subliminal consciousness" we see manifested in the psychic state, and natural somnambulism. Clairvoyance, psychometry, thought transference, etc., are as so many spectrum rays of the one soul light. Call them "subliminal" if you will. These rays flow out from the soul, and are many-hued, distinct or blurred, according to the degree of pureness or super-sensitivity of the external corporeal prism through which they are projected.

Persons have lived for years, we are credibly informed, who have spent half their lives entranced, *in the alternation of two distinct individualities* or two distinct states of consciousness, in one of which they forget all they had learned or did in the other.

Professor Huxley described (British Association of Science, Belfast, 1874) a case in which two separate lives, a normal, and abnormal one, seemed to be lived at intervals by the same individual during the greater portion of her life.

The conclusion to the whole matter is—the psychic, or soul-powers in some persons are less entrammelled by the senses than in others; that a high degree of organic sensitiveness always accompanies those who are recognised as psychics or sensitives; that this state of sensitiveness is natural to some, and in others may be developed by accident, disease, or induced by somnambulism and trance.

I will endeavour to show these psychic characteristics, or soul gifts, underlie, and enter into the varied phenomena—clairvoyance, psychometry, thought transference, thought-reading, and what not, which are collated under the title of,

"HOW TO THOUGHT-READ."

CHAPTER II.

CLAIRVOYANCE.

WHAT is clairvoyance? "The term, clairvoyance," says Dr. George Wyld, in a paper read before the Psychical Research Society, London, "is French, and means *clear-seeing*, but it appears to me to be an inadequate term, because it might signify clear optical vision, or clear mental vision. What is signified by the term is the power which certain individuals possess of seeing external objects under circumstances which render the sight of these objects impossible to physical optics. In short, by clairvoyance, we mean the power which the *mind* has of seeing or knowing thoughts and psychical conditions, and objects hidden from or beyond the reach of the physical senses; and if the existence of this faculty can be established, we arrive at a demonstration that man has a power within his body as yet unrecognised by physical science—a power which is called soul, or mind-seeing, and for the description of such a power the term might be auto-nocticy (αυτονοητικος), or psychoscopy." Psychoscopy, or soul sight, would, perhaps, be the better term. I propose to use the old term—clairvoyance—as it signifies, in popular usage, the power of seeing beyond the range of physical vision, as we know it.

That certain persons are endowed with this faculty of clear seeing—in some of its various phases—is a matter settled beyond dispute. What special name to call this faculty, or what are the true causes of its existence; why it should be possessed by some persons and not by others; why it should be so frail and fugitive in the presence of some people, and strong and vivid before others; why some persons are never clairvoyant until they have been through the mesmeric and psychic states; why some become possessed of the faculty through disease; while, with others, the gift of clairvoyance appears to be a spontaneous possession; and why some operators are successful in inducing clairvoyance, and others not, etc., are interesting questions to which the student of psychology may, with advantage, direct his attention.

Clairvoyance is soul-sight—the power of the soul to see. It is the state of refined psychic perception. This state increases in lucidity—clearness and power of penetration—in proportion as the activity of the physical senses are reduced below normal action. It is observed to be most effective in the trance state—natural or induced—as in the mesmeric and psychic states. I conclude, then, clairvoyance depends upon the unfolding of the spirit's perception, and is increased in power as the ascendency of the spirit arises above the activities of the spirit's corporeal envelope—the body. In proportion to the spirit's ascendency over the organs and senses of the body, is this psychic gift perfect or imperfect.

The large brain or cerebrum is the physical organ of the soul, as the cerebellum is of the physiological brain functions. Mental functions are manifested by the former, and physical functions by the latter.

Clairvoyance, as a spiritual faculty, will doubtless have its appropriate organ in the brain. I do not profess to locate that organ. At the same time I have noticed the best clairvoyants are wide and full between the eyes, showing there is a particular fulness of the frontal cerebral lobes, at their juncture at the root of the nose. This may be something more than a mere physiognomic sign. When this sign is accompanied by refinement of organisation, and a fine type of brain, I always look for the possible manifestation of clairvoyance in mesmeric subjects.

Some writers are of the opinion clairvoyance is actually soul-sight, more or less retarded in lucidity by the action or activity of the bodily senses. Others believe it to be a state arising from a peculiar highly-strained nervous condition, which induces the state of super-sensitivity or impressionability of the organisation. The first may be termed the spiritual, and the latter the physiological hypothesis. But, as a matter of fact, both conditions are noted. The latter may account for much, and possibly is sufficient to explain much that is called thought-reading—so often mistaken for clairvoyance. It does appear to me that certain peculiar physiological conditions, varying from semi-consciousness to profound trance, are necessary for the manifestation of clairvoyance, even when it takes place in apparently normal life of the possessor.

It is more than likely that the ornate and mystic ceremonies indulged in by Hindoo mystics, Egyptian, Grecian, and Roman priests, had the one grand end in view—viz., to induce the requisite state of super-sensitivity, and thus prepare the consecrated youths, sybils, and vestal virgins for the influx of spiritual vision, prophecy, and what not. When this subtle influx came—by whatever name called—the phenomena manifested were pretty much the same as we know them, only varied in degree. The gods spoke per oracle, Pythean, or Delphic. The man of God either coronated a king or foretold the end of a dynasty. St. Stephen saw Christ, St. John beheld visions, Joan of Arc was directed, Swedenborg illumined, and religious ecstatics in ancient and modern times partook more or less of the sacred fire—the inner sight. This (stripped of the fantastic surroundings, priestly mummeries, and dominant belief of the times) simply indicated the evolution and exercise of clairvoyance and other psychic gifts.

Coming nearer home, we hear of the mysterious visions at the Knock, and at Lourdes. Miraculous appearances of the Virgin and winged angels, to cheer the hearts of the faithful, and to cause the heads of the scornful to rejoice in sceptical derision. Then we have all the vagaries produced by the high nervous tension of modern revivalism, in which the visions seen are but a transformation of church and chapel dogmas into objective realities. These illusionary visions—mistaken for clairvoyance—possess less reality than the delusive fancies of the sensitive in the state of hypnosis.

Clairvoyance will be governed by its own spiritual laws, just as sight is affected or retarded by physical conditions. What these spiritual laws are we can only surmise, but this we may safely conjecture—viz., that soul-sight is not trammelled or limited by the natural laws which govern physical optics. Clairvoyance and physical vision are absolutely distinct, and possess little in common.

To illustrate a new subject, it is permissible to draw upon the old and the well-known. So I venture to illustrate clairvoyance by certain facts in connection with ordinary human vision. Although some children see better than others, the power to see, with the ability to understand the relative positions and uses of the things seen, is a matter of development. In psychic vision, we also see growth or development, with increasing power to use and understand the faculty. Some children are blind from birth, and others, seeing, lose the power of sight. Many are *blind*, although they have physical sight, they see not with *the educated eye*. Many, again, have greater powers of sight than they are aware of. As so it is with psychic vision.

What is true of the physical is also true of the psychic. From the first glimmerings, to the possession of well-defined sight, a period of growth and time elapses. From the first incoherent cry of infancy to well defined and intelligent speech of manhood, we notice the same agencies at work. Not only is clairvoyant vision generally imperfect at first, but the psychic's powers of description are also at fault. St. Paul could not give utterance to what he saw, when caught up to the third heavens. His knowledge of things and powers of speech failed him to describe the startling, the new, and the unutterable. He had a sudden revelation of the state of things in a sphere which had no counterparts in his previous experience, in this—his known—world. Hence, although he knew of his change of state, he could give no lawful or intelligible expression to his thoughts.

Between the first incongruous utterances, and apparent fantastic blunderings, and the more mature period in which "things spiritual" can be suitably described in our language, to our right sense of things, or comprehension, a period of development and education must elapse. It is true some clairvoyants develop much more readily than others.

In the entrancement of the mesmeric and psychic states, there is a lack of external consciousness. The soul is so far liberated from the body as to act independently of the ordinary sensuous conditions of the body, and sees by the perception and light of the inner or spiritual world, as distinct from the perception and light of this external or physical world. Elevated, or rather, liberated into this new condition, the clairvoyant loses connection with the thrums and threads of the physical organism, and is unable, or forgets for a time, how to speak of things as they are, or as they would appear to the physical vision of another. It is not surprising that in the earlier stages of clairvoyant development, and consequent transfer of ordinary consciousness and sensuous perception to that of spiritual consciousness and perception, the language of the clairvoyant should appear peculiar, incongruous, and "wanting," according to our ideas of clearness and precision.

One important lesson may be learned from this—viz., the operator should never force results, or strive to develop psychic perception by short cuts. Time must be allowed to the sensitive, for training and experience, and the development of self-confidence and expression.

Clairvoyance is not a common possession. Nevertheless, I believe there are many persons who possess the faculty unknown to themselves. By following out patiently, for a time, the requisite directions, the possession of this invaluable psychic gift might be discovered by many who now appear totally devoid of any clairvoyant indications. Its cultivation is possible and, in many ways, desirable.

"The higher attainment," says Dr. John Hamlin Davey, "of occult knowledge and power, the development of intuition, the psychometric sense, clairvoyant vision, inner hearing, etc., etc., thus reached, so open the avenues to a higher education, and enlarge the boundaries of human consciousness and activity, as to fairly dwarf into insignificance the achievements of external science."

Clairvoyance is as old as mankind, but the exhibition of clairvoyance, induced by mesmeric processes, was first announced by Puysegeur, a favourite pupil of Mesmer, in 1784. Since that time to the present not only have remarkable cases of clairvoyance cropped up, but there have been few mesmerists of any experience who have not had numerous cases under observation. Clairvoyance converted Dr. John Elliotson, F.R.S., one of the most scientific of British physicians, from extreme materialistic views to that of belief in soul and immortality. The same may be said of the late Dr. Ashburner, who was one of the Queen's physicians. Dr. Georget, author of "Physiology of the Nervous System,"—who was at one time opposed to a belief in the existence of a transcendental state in man,—found upon examination of the facts and incidents of artificial somnambulism, that *his materialism must go*. In his last will and testament, referring to the above-mentioned work, he says:—"This work had scarcely appeared, when renewed meditations on a very extraordinary phenomenon, somnambulism, no longer permitted me to entertain doubts of the existence within us, and external to us, of an intelligent principle, altogether different from material existences; in a word, of the soul and God. With respect to this I have a profound conviction, founded upon facts which I believe to be incontestable." Dr. Georget directed this change of opinion should have full publicity after his death.

Space would not suffice me to mention the names of all the highly educated and refined minds, in the medical, literary, philosophic, and scientific walks of life, who have studied these phenomena, and who, like

Dr. Georget, have no more doubts of their reality than they have of their own physical existence, status, or reputation. Among medical men—some of whom I have known and corresponded with—might be mentioned Sir James Simpson, Drs. Elliotson, Ashburner, Esdaile, Buss, Garth Wilkinson, Hands, Wyld, Hitchman, Eadon, and Davey. Among others on the roll of fame, might be noticed Archbishop Whately; Earls Ducie, Stanhope, Macclesfield, Charleville; the present Duke of Argyle; Lord R. Cavendish, Lord Lindsay; Burton, the traveller; and the late Sergeant Cox. Among literary men, Mr. Gladstone, Britain's foremost statesman and scholar; Mr. Balfour, his able and talented opponent; Bulwer Lytton, Marryat, Neal, Robert Chambers, Dickens, and Stevenson, of "Dr. Jekyll and Mr. Hyde" fame. Mr. George Combe, the distinguished Scottish metaphysician, philosopher, author, phrenologist, etc., was profoundly interested in the phenomena. Among well-known men of science might be mentioned Camille Flammarion, the French astronomer; Fichte, the German philosopher; Professors Tornebom and Edland, Swedish physicists; Professor Oliver Lodge, D.Sc., F.R.S.; Alfred Russell Wallace, D.C.L., LL.D.; William Crookes, F.R.S.; Cromwell F. Varley, F.R.S. Notwithstanding this somewhat formidable array of investigators of clairvoyance, many good people will not hesitate to deny the value of such evidence, and yet will believe anything in its favour which may be found in the Bible, as to its existence in the *past*. It is a strange perversion of judgment—not at all surprising—when the majority take (second-hand) for their religious(?) views whatever is recognised as "sound" in each particular district and Church. It is not a question of belief, it is "a question of evidence," as Mr. Gladstone avers.

The Rev. Mr. M'Kinnon, late pastor of Chalmers' Free Church, Glasgow, told me a short time ago, "Clairvoyance was nothing more than a high nervous concentrated form of mental vision," to which I replied, "Admitting the hypothesis—which, however, explained nothing—it matters little what clairvoyance is esteemed to be or called, if the facts connected with it are acknowledged." Even this friend admitted he knew a man in Mull, who lived on the half croft, next to his father's croft. This man had great repute in that district as "having the Second Sight." Whatever this man foretold always came to pass. One instance will suffice. He (Mr. M'Kinnon) remembered that one day, while this crofter (who was a tailor by trade) was working, he suddenly stopped, and looked *out into vacancy*—

as he always did when the "Second Sight was on him"—and described a funeral coming over the hill, the mourners, who they were, and numbers, the way the procession took, and the name of the "man whose face was covered," and finally, when the procession would appear. Mr. M'Kinnon's parents noted the time, and being simple Highland folk, accustomed to the accuracy of this man's visions, they believed what he said, and kept his saying in their hearts till the time of fulfilment came about. Mr. M'Kinnon assured me "the funeral took place to the day and hour, twelve months subsequently to the vision, as predicted." All I can say is, if "a high nervous concentrated form of mental vision" is capable of pointing out all this, it is worthy of investigation. It is evident this tailor at least had a power of vision—prevoyance—not of the ordinary, everyday kind of vision. Second sight, as exhibited in this case, is what may be termed spontaneous clairvoyance.

Epes Sargent, in his work, "The Scientific Basis of Spiritualism," referring to clairvoyance, says: "As far as I have admitted it as part of a scientific basis (demonstrating man's spiritual nature), it is the exercise of the supersensual faculty of penetrating opaque and dense matter as if by the faculty of sight. But it does more. It detects our unuttered, undeveloped thoughts; it goes back along the past, and describes what is hidden; nay, the proofs are overwhelming that it may pierce the future, and predict coming events from the shadows they cast before.

"What is it that sees without the physical eyes, and without the assistance of light? What is normal sight? It is not the vibrating ether—it is not the external eye—that sees. It is the soul using the eye as an instrument, and light as a condition. Prove once that sight can exist without the use of light, sensation, or any physical organ of vision, and you prove an abnormal, supersensual, spiritual faculty—a proof which puts an end to the theory of materialism, and which, through its affinity with analogous or corresponding facts, justifies its introduction as part of a scientific basis for the spiritual theory."

J. F. Deleuze was profoundly convinced of the existence of this faculty. He claimed that the power of seeing at a distance, prevision, and the transference of thought without the aid of external signs, were in themselves sufficient proofs of the existence of spirituality of soul.

Except in a very few instances, little or no pains are taken to cultivate the spiritual nature of man. Civilised man of to-day is but rising out of the age of brute force of yesterday, and he is still circumscribed by love of earthly power and position. He is an acquisitive rather than a spiritual being. Being dominated by the senses, he will naturally seek and appreciate that which gratifies his senses most. He has little time or patience for anything which does not contribute pleasure to his sensuous nature. He would give time to the investigation of the soul side of life if it brought gold, the means of enjoyment, and gratified his acquisitiveness and love of power. Probably the majority give the subject no attention at all. If the spiritual side of our natures were as fully cultivated as those elements which bring us bread and butter and praise of men in the market-place, there is no doubt, no manner of doubt whatever, but the most of us would occupy a nobler and more spiritually elevated plane in life; and were adequate means taken, I doubt not but this faculty of clairvoyance would become more generally known and cultivated. Even to the selfish, worldly and non-spiritual man, clairvoyance is not without its practical side and utility, such, for instance, as supplying Chicago with water. To the spiritually minded, clairvoyance and all psychic gifts are appreciated, less for what they will bring, than for the testimony they present of man's spiritual origin, transcendental powers and probable continuity of life beyond this mortal vale.

CHAPTER III.

CLAIRVOYANCE ILLUSTRATED.

CLAIRVOYANCE may be briefly classified as far and near, direct and indirect, objective and subjective. I propose to give a few well-authenticated cases to illustrate these phases in this chapter.

FAR AND DIRECT CLAIRVOYANCE

is possibly the highest and purest combination. The sensitive is able to state facts not within the range of the knowledge of those present. Thus when Swedenborg described to the Queen and her friends, when at a distance of several hundred miles from the conflagration, the burning of her palace at Christiania, no one present could possibly know of the fire or the incidents connected therewith. Hence no thought-reading, brain-picking, much less guess-work or coincidence, could account for the exactness of details given by the seer. Clairvoyance in this case was not only far and direct, but objective. That is, the matter recorded was connected with the physical or objective plane.

CLAIRVOYANCE AN AID TO SCIENCE.

"Chicago, as is well-known, is one of the most go-ahead cities in the world. Like Jonah's gourd it appeared to spring up in a night. Its population rapidly increased, and water soon became a *sine qua non*, both as regards use and luxury. Science was at fault; for geologists had pronounced that there could be no water beneath such a strata. Top water was all that could be looked for, and presently a water company was formed to supply this impure kind of liquid.

"There happened to live at this time in Chicago a person named Abraham James, a simple-minded man, of Quaker descent, uneducated, and in fact, quite an ignorant person. It was discovered by a Mrs. Caroline Jordon that James was a natural clairvoyant, in fact a medium, and that he had declared when put into the trance condition that both water and petroleum, in large quantities, would be found in a certain tract of land in the neighbourhood of the city. For a long time no attention was paid to his statements. At length two gentlemen from Maine, called Whitehead and Scott, coming to Chicago on business, and hearing what had been said by Abraham James, had him taken to the land where he said water could be had in immense quantities by boring for. Being entranced, James at once pointed out the very spot. He told them that he not only saw the water, but could trace its source from the Rocky Mountains, 2000 miles away, to the spot on which they stood, and could sketch out on maps the strata and caverns through which it ran. Negotiations were at once entered into for the purchase of the land, and the work of boring was commenced. This was in February, 1864, and the process went on daily till November, when, having reached a depth of 711 feet, water was struck, and flowed up at once at the rate of 600,000 gallons every 24 hours.

"The borings showed the following kinds of strata passed through by the drill, and this was spiritually seen and described by the clairvoyant as practical proofs to the senses of other people. First the drill passed through alluvium soil, 100 feet; limestone, saturated with oil, 35 feet, which would burn as well as any coal; Joliet marble, 100 feet; conglomerate strata of sand and flint, mixed with iron pyrites and traces of copper, 125 feet; rock (shale) saturated with petroleum, the sediment coming up like putty, thick and greasy, 156 feet; galena limestone was next reached at a depth of 530 feet; a bed of limestone, containing flint and sulphuret of iron was bored through, the depth being 639 feet, and being very hard, the work went on slowly. At this point there appeared a constant commotion arising from the escape of gas, the water suddenly falling from 30 to 60 feet, and then as suddenly rising to the surface, carrying with it chippings from the drill, and other matters. The work still went on; when at the depth of 711 feet the arch of the rock was penetrated, and the water suddenly burst forth from a bore 4½ in. at the bottom, of a temperature of 58° F., clear as crystal, pure as diamond, and perfectly free from every kind of animal and vegetable matter, and which, for drinking purposes and health, is much better adapted than any water yet known, and will turn out to be the poor man's friend for all time to come.

"Here, then, is a huge fact for the faithless: the fact brought to light by dynamic or invisible agency, and which no power of negation can gainsay.

Natural science said, No water could be found; but psychology said—False, for I will point out the spot where it will flow in splendid streams as long as the earth spins on its axis. Since 1864 the artesian well of Chicago has poured forth water at the rate of a million and a half gallons daily; and what is economic, to say nothing of Yankee shrewdness, it is conveyed into ponds or reservoirs which in winter freeze, producing 40,000 tons of ice for sale, and which might be quadrupled at any time."[B] This is a case of far and near, direct and objective clairvoyance. This historical incident proves the value and reality of psychic vision.

Indirect clairvoyance is the power of discerning what may be more or less in the minds of those present, including absent or forgotten thoughts and incidents. Thus, when a clairvoyant describes a place with accuracy, recognised by some one present to be correct, and also gives details partly known and unknown, but afterwards found to be correct, this mixture of phases may be recognised as indirect.

SUBJECTIVE CLAIRVOYANCE

is that phase which enables the sensitive to perceive things and ideas on the spiritual or subjective plane. The late Rev. Stainton Moses, well known in literary circles as "M.A., Oxon," once asked the following pertinent questions:—"Is there conceivably a mass of life all round us of which most of us have no cognisance? One gifted lady I know sees clairvoyantly the spirit-life of all organised things, of a tree or plant for example. I have heard her describe what her interior faculties perceive. Is it a fact that spirit, underlying everything, can be so perceived by the awakened faculties?" I should say yes. If this lady's clairvoyance has been of a high order in other respects—why not in this? This type of psychic vision is of the subjective order.

There are necessarily an infinite variety of phases, pure and mixed, which the investigator will meet in practice. These phases may be called *far*, such as seeing objects, etc., at a distance—prevoyance, predicting events; retrovoyance, reading the past; introvoyance, seeing internally, or examining bodies, as in disease; external introvoyance, seeing into lockets, packets, letters, safes, and discovering hidden, known or forgotten, or lost objects. Lastly, there is pseudo-clairvoyance. For one case of direct there are hundreds of well authenticated cases of indirect clairvoyance, and again for one of the latter there are thousands of pseudo-clairvoyance, which are the outcome of states similar to hypnosis, and are nothing more than an incongruous medley of suggested ideas and fancies. Thus a strong and positive willed person can impinge his ideas through the thought-atmosphere of the sensitive and distort or deflect the psychic vision, and render abortive any attempts to get beyond the circle of the dominating influence. Again, the sensitive may enter a realm of fancy—a veritable dreamland of coherent and incoherent ideation, either the product of the sensitive's own condition, or of suggestion—accidental, spontaneous, and determined—in the sensitive's surroundings. Of course any classification of the numerous phases of clairvoyance must be purely arbitrary.

DIRECT AND OBJECTIVE CLAIRVOYANCE—LOST GOODS RESTORED.

This instance of far vision is taken from "A Tangled Yarn," page 173, "Leaves from Captain James Payn's Log," which was published recently by C. H. Kelly. As I knew Captain Hudson, of Swansea, personally, and heard from his own lips the following incident, I have much pleasure in introducing it here as a further illustration of the *Cui bono* of clairvoyance:—

"The *Theodore* got into Liverpool the same day as the *Bland*. She was a larger ship than ours but had a similar cargo. The day that I went to the owners to report 'all right,' I met with Captain Morton in a terrible stew because he was thirty bales of cotton short, a loss equal to the whole of his own wages and the mate's into the bargain. He was so fretted over it that his wife in desperation recommended him to get the advice of a Captain Hudson, who had a young female friend clever as a clairvoyant. We were both sceptical in the matter of clairvoyance. At first Morton didn't wish to meddle, he said, with 'a parcel of modern witchcraft,' and that sort of thing; but he at last yielded to his wife's urgency and consented to go. There was first of all a half-crown fee to Captain Hudson, and then the way was clear for an interview with the young clairvoyant. I was present to 'see fair.' When the girl had been put into the clairvoyant state Morton was instructed to take her right hand in his right hand and ask her any questions he wished. The replies were in substance as follows:—She went back mentally to the port whence the *Theodore* had sailed, retracing with her hand as she in words also described the course of the ship from Liverpool across the Atlantic, through the West Indian group, etc., back to New Orleans. At length she said, 'Yes, this is the place where the cotton was lost; it's put on board a big black ship with a red mark round it.' Then she began to trace with her hand and describe the homeward course of the vessel, but after re-crossing the Atlantic, instead of coming up the Irish Channel for Liverpool, she turned along the English Channel as though bound for the coast of France; and then stretching out her hand she exclaimed, 'Oh, here's the cotton; but what funny people they are; they don't talk English.' Captain Morton said at once, 'I see; it's the *Brunswick*, Captain Thomas,' an American ship that lay alongside of him at New Orleans and was taking in her cargo of cotton while the *Theodore* was loading, and was bound for Havre de Grace. Captain Morton, satisfied with his clairvoyant's information, went home and wrote immediately to Captain Thomas, inquiring for his lost cargo. In due course he got an answer that the cotton was certainly there, that it had been taken off the wharf in mistake, and that it was about to be sold for whomsoever it might concern; but that if he (Captain Morton) would remit a certain amount to cover freight and expenses the bales should be forwarded to him at once. He did so, and in due time received the cotton, subject only to the expenses of transit from Havre to Liverpool. Such are the facts; I do not profess to offer any explanation."

CLAIRVOYANCE AN AID TO THE PHYSICIAN.

I am indebted to Dr. George Wyld for this case, which also exhibits the value of clairvoyance. Dr. Wyld had the good fortune to make the acquaintance of a Mrs. D——, a lady in private life who was endowed with the gift of natural clairvoyance. Dr. Wyld told this lady of "a friend who had for years suffered intense agony for hours every night in his back and chest, and that latterly he had been obliged to sit up all night in a chair, and his legs began to swell."

"This gentleman had regularly for three years been under many of the leading physicians of London. Some said that there must be some obscure heart affection, others said it was neuralgia, one said it was gout, and the last consulted said it was malignant caries of the spine."

Dr. Wyld's friend called upon him by appointment, and met Mrs. D——. This lady merely looked at him. When he had retired from the room Mrs. D—— made the following statement of his case to the doctor:—"I have seen what the disease is; I saw it as distinctly as if the body were transparent. There is a tumour behind the heart, about the size of a walnut; it is of a dirty colour; and it jumps and looks as if it would burst. Nothing can do him any good but entire rest."

"I at once saw," says Dr. Wyld, what she meant, and sat down to write to my friend's medical attendant as follows:—

"I believe I have discovered the nature of Mr.——'s disease. He has an aneurism on the descending aorta, about the size of a walnut. It is this which causes the slight displacement which has been observed in the heart, and the pressure of the tumour against the intercostal nerves is the cause of the agony in the back, and the peripheral pains in the front of the chest. You are going to-morrow to see Sir —— in consultation; show him this diagnosis, and let me know what he says."

"Next the patient had the consultation, and Mrs. D——'s diagnosis was confirmed; and the doctors agreed with Mrs. D—— the only thing to be done was to take entire rest. The treatment was duly followed up, with successful results." Dr. Wyld thoughtfully adds—"It is true that the diagnosis cannot be absolutely confirmed during life, but as the profession unanimously pronounce the disease to be aneurism, the diagnosis may be accepted as correct. This diagnosis has probably saved the gentleman's life, as before Mrs. D—— saw him he was allowed to shoot over Scotch moors, and to ride, drive, and play billiards."

The use of clairvoyance in the diagnosis of disease is by no means as rare as the majority of physicians and the general public would naturally assume. I have had many opportunities of witnessing the accuracy of diagnosis and the excellence of the methods of treatment advised by clairvoyants. In my own personal experience I have had much evidence of correctness of clairvoyance in diagnosis, and subsequent success in treatment. It is a phase most desirable to cultivate if possible, and all allied conditions connected therewith.

TRAVELLING CLAIRVOYANCE.

As a public entertainer at one time, giving demonstrations of mesmeric phenomena, I have had naturally many opportunities of seeing different types of clairvoyance. During a course of entertainments given by me in Rothesay, 1881, I was able to introduce clairvoyance to public notice by the most difficult method, that of public experiments.

M. C., the clairvoyante, was a native of Newcastle-on-Tyne. All her clairvoyant experiments were satisfactory. Her husband was also a clairvoyant, but not so striking for public exhibition. M. C. seemed to possess all phases. One or two experiments out of many will be interesting not only as illustrative of clairvoyance, but because what I relate can be easily ratified.

M. C. arrived in Rothesay for the first time about four hours previously to taking her seat upon the platform, in the New Public Halls. It was neither possible nor probable she could have obtained the information she possessed by other than psychic means. The clairvoyant was mesmerised and blindfolded before the audience. After some experiments in objective clairvoyance were given, such as describing a watch, telling the time, and the number, by having the watch held silently over her forehead, she gave several experiments in travelling clairvoyance. Many visitors in the hall—for Rothesay is a well known and fashionable seaside resort—sent up requests to the platform, and desired the clairvoyante should visit their homes in Kent, Cornwall, Island of Jersey, in the Isle of Man, Glasgow, and other places. Her visits and descriptions were in all instances extremely satisfactory. How far thought-transference and objective clairvoyance commingled and entered into her descriptions it would be difficult to say, but the results were simply marvellous.

Test case, by the late Dr. Maddever, M.D., M.R.C.S., and Dr. John Maddever, his son. These medical gentlemen resided in Rothesay, and were present in the hall. Dr. Maddever desired me to send the clairvoyante into a certain room in his house and that she should describe it.

All the directions the clairvoyante obtained were, "to go out of the hall, down the front steps; when out turn to the right and proceed onward till she came to an iron-railed gate, on which was a small brass plate, bearing the name of 'Dr. Maddever,' she was to open the gate, go up to the hall-door, enter, pass the first door to the left, and turn round a passage to the left and enter the first door to which she came, and describe what she saw."

Sitting still upon the platform in silence for a minute or two, she suddenly exclaimed:—"I am at the gate—at the door—now in the hall—I have found the room, and I am now inside, and stand with my back to the door." She then proceeded to describe the room, the book-cases which surrounded it, their peculiar structure; the mantel-piece, the form of the clock, the time, and the appearance of the ornaments. The table in the centre of the room, its form, the colour and style of the cloth upon it, books, albums, and papers thereon, the flower vase support in the window, and a number of other particulars.

At the conclusion Dr. Maddever arose in the audience and said:—"Ladies and gentlemen, Professor Coates is a stranger to me, I only know of him by report. The young lady on the platform I do not know. I have not seen either till this evening, and they have never been in my house. The experiment we have had is most remarkable, and should be of deep and profound interest to all. The young lady has described the room, as far as I can remember, most correctly—in fact very much better than I could have done myself." This statement was received with applause.

After one or two instances of travelling clairvoyance, a young gentleman rose in the body of the hall and desired I should send the sensitive to a house or villa not far from the juncture of Marine Place and Ardbeg Road.

The directions given to the clairvoyante were briefly to the effect, she was to leave the place, on reaching the front street she was to turn to her left and keep on past the Post Office, Esplanade, past the Skeoch Woods, etc., till she came to the house. She nodded her head in compliance, and presently announced she "had found the house." Then she shivered and appeared to draw back, and said "I won't go in."

Some persons in the audience laughed, and one (I think it was the young gentleman who asked that she might be sent) said: "The whole thing is a swindle." Now, considering there was not a single flaw in the experiments that night, surprise after surprise being given, and the audience had risen in enthusiasm, this opinion was not favourably received.

I asked the gentleman "to have patience." I had no doubt but we would know soon enough the reasons. "Whatever they were I would try and ascertain them."

With much hesitancy she declared that "the house was not one any respectable female would enter, and she would not." When I repeated this statement to the audience, there was what the newspapers call "sensation." The sensation was intensified when one of the Rothesay Magistrates, Bailie Molloy, the then senior Bailie of the Royal Burgh, declared "the young woman was right, perfectly right, this was a house which had been inadvertently let to persons of ill-fame, and he, for one, had recently had the facts of the case placed before him, and he was most anxious that these people should be put out, and they would be, as soon as the proper steps could be taken."

The young gentleman retired somewhat discomfited, and the excitement produced by these and other experiments brought crowded houses during my professional stay.

When my "mesmeric exposition" was concluded, the two medical gentlemen referred to, were good enough to introduce themselves, and invited me to call next day to see the room. I accepted the invitation during the following day and saw how truly correct and vivid her description had been. In the first experiment the sensitive described the state of the doctor's library, pointing out what had not been recollected by either of the medical men, and I believe the other case comes under the heading of direct and objective clairvoyance. Dr. Maddever's house was about a quarter of a mile, and the other house about a mile and a half from the hall.

The persistent and reliable clairvoyance evinced by this sensitive was induced. She was a mesmeric subject, and when such subjects are properly treated they make the very best clairvoyants.

PSYCHIC VISION POSSESSED BY THE PHYSICALLY BLIND.

Mrs. Croad resided at Redland, Bristol. My attention was called to her case about fifteen years ago by Dr. J. G. Davey, of Bristol. Unfortunately circumstances at the time prevented a personal visit and report. Her psychic gifts and wonderful supersensitivity have been amply testified to, by most reliable witnesses, such as Dr. Davey, Hy. G. Atkinson, F.G.S., and others.

Clairvoyance in Mrs. Croad's case was and is (for I believe the lady is still living) a singular admixture of subtle sense transference so well known to mesmerists of the old school, and spontaneous psychic vision. Thought-transference and indirect clairvoyance, more or less induced, by intense voluntary concentration.

Mrs. Croad is deaf, dumb, and paralysed, and stone blind. She can see and hear, read with powers "denied to ordinary mortals," and discern pictures and writings in the dark. She is aware of her daughter's thoughts when the latter touches her, and becomes at once acquainted with what her daughter wishes to communicate. She possesses supersensitivity of touch, and discerns colour by their degrees of heat, roughness or smoothness. She can also identify photographs and pictures in the same way. From time to time she has exhibited the highest phases of clairvoyance. Reports have been made in this case by medical experts in the *Journal of Psychological Medicine*, and other magazines and journals several years ago. The most recent was contributed by the Rev. Taliesin Dans, The Cottage, Claptons, to *The Review of Reviews* in January, 1891.

THE SPIRITUALISTIC AND PRACTICAL CHARACTER OF CLAIRVOYANCE

might be further illustrated by the well known case of Miss Eliza Hamilton, who became paralysed in her limbs and right arm, through severe injury to the spine. She had been in hospital for four months, on her return home frequently passed into the trance state, and on awakening described various people and places she had visited, and objects seen. These descriptions have been invariably verified subsequently. "She also at times," says her physician, "speaks of having been in the company of persons with whom she was acquainted in this world, but who have passed away; and she tells her friends that they have become more beautiful, and have cut off their infirmities with which they were afflicted while here. She often describes events which *are about to happen*, and these are always fulfilled exactly as she predicts."

"Her father," says Mr. Hudson Tuttle, "read in her presence a letter he had received from a friend in Leeds, speaking of the loss of his daughter, about whose fate he was very unhappy, as she had disappeared nearly a month before, and left no trace. Eliza went into the trance state, and cried out, 'Rejoice! I have found the lost girl! She is happy in the angel world.' She said the girl had fallen into the dark water where dyers washed their cloths; that her friends could not have found her had they sought her there, *but* now the body had floated a few miles, and would be found in the River Aire. The body was found as described.

"Now, knowing that her eyes were closed, that she could not hear, that her bodily senses were in profound lethargy, how are we to account for the intensity and keenness of sight? Her mental powers were exceedingly exalted, and scarcely a question could be asked her but she correctly answered.

"In this case the independence of the mind of the physical body are shown in every instance of clairvoyance, is proven beyond cavil or doubt. If it is demonstrated that the mind sees without the aid of eyes, hears when the ears are deaf, feels when the nerves of sensation are at rest, it follows that it is independent of these outward avenues, and has other channels of communication with the external world essentially its own."

CLAIRVOYANCE FROM DISEASE.

Miss Mollie Fancher, of Brooklyn Heights, fell off a tramway car when eighteen years of age, experienced very severe injuries to head and spine, her body being dragged a distance, through her dress catching on the step of the car. She became paralysed, lost all her senses, except touch. She gradually recovered hearing, taste, and ability to talk in time. She was also blind for nine years. Drs. Speir and Ormiston were her physicians, men of skill and marked probity. These, with a veritable host of medical men—ministers of the Gospel, educationists and specialists—have borne testimony to her remarkable endowments, from which we take two extracts. Mr. Charles Ewart, Principal of the Brooklyn Heights Seminary, where she was under special care, writes:—

"For many days together she has been to all appearances dead. The slightest pulse could not be detected; there was no evidence of respiration. Her limbs were as cold as ice, and had there not been some warmth about her heart, she would have been buried. When I first saw her she had but one sense—that of touch. By running her fingers over the printed page, she could read with equal facility in light or darkness. The most delicate work is done by her in the night.... Her power of clairvoyance, or second sight, is marvellously developed. *Distance imposes no barriers,* without the slightest error she dictates the contents of sealed letters which have never been in her hands. She discriminates in darkness the most delicate shades of colour. She writes with extraordinary rapidity."

Mr. Henry M. Parkhurst, the astronomer (residing at 173 Gates Avenue, Brooklyn, N.Y.), writes:—

"From the waste-basket of a New York gentleman acquaintance he fished an unimportant business letter, without reading it, tore it into ribbons, and tore the ribbons into squares. He shook the pieces well together, put them into an envelope, and sealed it. This he subsequently handed to Miss Fancher. The blind girl took the envelope in her hand, and passed her hand over it several times, called for paper and pencil, and wrote it verbatim. The seal of the letter had not been broken. Mr. Parkhurst himself opened it, pasted the contents together, and compared the two. Miss Fancher's was a literal copy of the original."

MESMERIC CLAIRVOYANCE AND SPIRITUALISM.

"A few evenings ago I called upon Mr. and Mrs. Loomis, 2 Vernon Place, Bloomsbury, and after we had chatted for a short time in the drawing-room with the door closed and nobody else present, I asked if they would try a mesmeric experiment for me. They willingly agreed, and Mr. Loomis, by passes, threw his wife into a mesmeric state, as he often does, and an intelligence, which claimed to be the spirit of her mother, spoke through her lips. Until this moment I had said nothing to any living soul about the nature of my contemplated experiment, but I then asked the unseen intelligence if it could then and there go to the house of Mrs. Macdougall Gregory, 21 Green Street, Grosvenor Square, London, and move a heavy physical object in her presence. The reply was, I do not know, I will try. About three minutes afterwards, at 8.40 p.m., the intelligence said that Mrs. Gregory was in her drawing-room with a friend, and added, 'I have made Mrs. Gregory feel a prickly sensation in her arm from the elbow down to the hand, as if some person had squeezed the arm, and she has spoken about it to her friend.'

"I took a note in writing of this statement at the time it was made. A few minutes later I left Mr. and Mrs. Loomis, and without telling them my intention to do so, went straight to the house of Mrs. Gregory about a mile and a half off. I had selected Mrs. Gregory for this experiment because she is not afraid to publish her name in connection with psychic truths, and her word carries weight, especially in Scotland, where she and her family are well-known. She is the widow of Professor Gregory, of Edinburgh University, and is a lineal descendant of the Lord of the Isles. I then for the first time told Mrs. Gregory of the experiment. She replied that between half-past eight and nine o'clock that evening she was playing the piano, and suddenly turned round to her friend, Miss Yauewicz, of Upper Norwood, saying, 'I don't know what is the matter with me, I feel quite stupid, and have such a pain in my right arm that I cannot go on playing.' Miss Yauewicz, who was no believer in spiritualism or any of the marvels of psychology, felt a lively interest when she was informed of the experiment. She told me that she clearly remembered Mrs. Gregory's statement that she could not go on playing because of the pain in her right arm."[C]

Mrs. Loomis was a remarkable clairvoyante, whom I accidently became acquainted with in Liverpool many years ago, shortly after her arrival from America. I introduced the lady and her husband, Mr. Daniel Loomis, to Mr. Harrison, then editor of *The Spiritualist*. The Guion steamer, *Idaho*, in which they came from New York, was wrecked off the Irish Coast, and all they possessed in this world was lost with the vessel. Mrs. Loomis predicted the disaster, where it was likely to take place; that all hands would be saved, but all they had lost. Upon the arrival of the officers of the vessel in Liverpool, they presented Mrs. Loomis, at the Bee Hotel, John Street, Liverpool, with a basket of flowers, purse, and testimonial, in recognition of her gift, and heroic conduct during and after the disaster. I may add I knew Mr. Harrison as a most careful investigator and a man of scientific tastes and ability.

I select the following case of a mesmeric sensitive controlled by a disembodied spirit, from the writings of Mr. Epes Sargent, author of "Planchette on the Despair of Science," etc., as appropriately illustrative of this form of clairvoyance:—

"One of the daughters of my valued correspondent, the late William Howett, was a mesmeric sensitive. Howett told Professor W. D. Gunning, whose words (slightly abridged) I here use, that, on one occasion his daughter, being entranced, wrote a communication signed with the name of her brother, supposed to be in Australia. The import was, that he had been drowned a few days before in a lake. Dates and details were given. The parents could only wait, as there was no trans-oceanic telegraph. Months passed, and at last a letter came from a nephew in Melbourne, bearing the tidings that their son had been drowned on such a day, in such a lake, under such and such circumstances. Date, place, and all the essential details were the same as those given months before through the daughter. Mr. Howett believed that the freed spirit of his son influenced the sister to write; and I know of no explanation more rational that this."

CLAIRVOYANCE DUE TO SPIRITUAL CONTROL.

Such cases as the above are the most difficult of all to prove. What I contend for is, if it is demonstrated we can control a fellow-being, throw him or her into a trance state—in which the phenomena of the psychic state are evolved—and seeing such state is induced largely by the control of spirit over spirit in the body, why may not a disembodied spirit control, direct, or influence a suitable sensitive or medium in the body? If not, why not? There is abundant evidence of such controls.

Seeing objects concealed in boxes and letters, or reading books and mottoes, etc., appears to some clairvoyants to be more difficult than diagnosing disease, or seeing objects at a distance. The why and wherefore seems at first difficult to explain.

The deliberate concealment of objects for the purpose of testing clairvoyance is often the result of a spirit of virulent suspicion, disbelief, and what is worse, *an earnest desire for failure,* so that the parties may rejoice on the discomfiture of the clairvoyants. With such people failure is a source of pleasure. Nevertheless, seeming impossibilities have been triumphed over. Long lost wills have been found, and places of the accidental or intentional hiding discovered. In more than one case deliberate fraud has been exposed, and the guilty parties brought to acknowledge the truth of the sensitive's revelations.

THE FUGITIVE NATURE OF CLAIRVOYANCE.

"The chief feature," said Alexis Didier, "of the somnambulistic lucidity is its variability. While the conjurer or juggler, at all moments in the day and before all spectators, will invariably succeed, the somnambulist, endowed with the marvellous power of clairvoyance, will not be lucid with all interviewers and at all moments of the day; for the faculty of lucidity being a crisis painful and abnormal, there may be atmospheric influences or invincible antipathies at work opposing its production, and which seem to paralyse all supersensual manifestation. Intuition, clairvoyance, lucidity, are faculties which the somnambulist gets from the nature of his temperament, and which are rarely developed in force." Further, he adds, "the somnambulistic lucidity varies in a way to make one despair; success is continually followed by failure; in a word, error succeeds a truth; but when one analyses the causes of this no right-minded person will bring up the charge of Charlatanism, since the faculty is subject to influences independent of the will and the consciousness of the clairvoyant."

Alexis Didier, like his brother Adolphe, was a natural clairvoyant, and excelled in direct and objective clairvoyance, phases of the most striking and convincing character.

Clairvoyance can be cultivated by the aid of mesmerism and by the introspection process. By the first, the sensitive can be materially assisted by the experience and help of the operator. By the second, something like natural clairvoyance can be induced. Either processes are more or less suitable to subdue the activity of the senses, and give greater range to the psychic powers. General instructions are of little use. Personal advice is best. The operator then knows with whom he has to do, their special temperament and character, what are the best processes to adopt to cultivate their gift, and how far such sensitives and students are themselves likely to be suitable for clairvoyant experiments. I have found the "Mirror Disc" useful in inducing favourable conditions in the normal state for the development of clairvoyance, and recommend its use.

CHAPTER IV.

Psychometry.

J. RHODES BUCHANAN, M.D.

WHAT is psychometry? Dr. George Wyld esteems psychometry a phase of clairvoyance—"the knowledge the psychic obtains by a *clue*, such as a lock of the hair of some absent person, or some portion of a distant object." Mr. Stead calls it (*Review of Reviews*, p. 221, September, 1892) "the strange new science of psychometry." In this he pardonably errs. Psychometry may be strange, but *it* is *not* new. We may not recognise the name as old, but the class of phenomena it specialises is as old as clairvoyance and mind-reading.

"The word psychometry," says Dr. Buchanan, "coined in 1842, to express the character of a new science and art, is the most pregnant and important word that has been added to the English language. Coined from the Greek (*psyche*, soul; and *metron*, measure), it literally signifies *soul-measuring*."... "The psychometer measures the soul."

In the case of psychometry, the measuring assumes a new character, as the object measured and the measuring instrument are the same psychic element, and its measuring power is not limited to the psychic, as it was developed in the first experiments, but has appeared by successive investigations to manifest a wider and wider area of power, until it became apparent that this psychic capacity was really the measure of all things in the universe. Hence, psychometry signifies not merely the measuring of souls and soul capacities, or qualities by our own psychic capacities, but the measurement and judgment of all things conceivable by the human mind; and psychometry means practically *measuring by the soul*, or grasping and estimating all things which are within the range of human intelligence. Psychometry, therefore, is not merely an instrumentality for measuring soul powers, but a comprehensive agency like mathematics for the solution of many departments of science.

"Prophecy," says Buchanan, "is the noblest aspect of psychometry, and there is no reason why it should not become the guiding power to each individual life, and the guiding power of the destiny of nations." For instance, while all Europe feared for Boulanger, Metz was getting stored with food; Lord Wolseley declared war imminent, and the French themselves prepared for *revanche*. Psychometers declared for peace in 1889, and said there was no prospect of war for five years. Subsequent events have proved Boulanger lacking in both generalship and statesmanship—a veritable Bombastes Furioso; and peace up to the time of writing is as yet unbroken.

Dr. Buchanan claims—"In physiology, pathology, and hygiene, psychometry is as wise and parental as in matters of character and ethics. A competent psychometer appreciates the vital forces, the temperament, the peculiarities, and every departure from the normal state, realising the diseased condition with an accuracy in which external diagnosis often fails. In fact, the natural psychometer is born with a genius for the healing art, and if the practice of medicine were limited to those who possess this power in an eminent degree, its progress would be rapid, and its disgraceful failures in diagnosis and blunders in treatment and prognosis would be less frequently heard of." Many happy tests in diagnosis and in the successful treatment of disease—out of the ordinary routine—are due, in my opinion, not so much to elaborate medical training as to the fact of the practitioner—perhaps unconscious to himself—being possessed of more or less of the psychometric faculty.

Dr. Buchanan,[D] in his "Original Sketch," gives us the history and some details of his discovery, based upon certain investigations of the nervous system. Already he was well versed in the phenomena of hypnotism, which is at this late day becoming a fashionable study and recreation of medical men. He had demonstrated the responsive action of cerebral organs to mesmeric touch and influence, and he was already acquainted with the curious psychological phenomena of sense and thought transference, of double consciousness, and all the nervous and pathological phases peculiar to natural and artificial somnambulism. His investigation for years of the nervous system had clearly shown him that its capacities were far more extensive, varied, and interesting than physiologists and philosophers either knew or were prepared to admit. He found in the nervous system a vast aggregate of powers which constitute the vitality of man, existing in intimate connection with the vast and wonderful powers of his mind. Was it possible or rational to suppose that this nerve-matter, so intimately co-related with mind, and upon which the mind depends for the manifestation of its powers, could be entirely limited to the narrow materialistic sphere assigned by physiologists? He thought not.

In a conversation with Bishop Polk (who afterwards became the celebrated General Polk of Confederate fame), Dr. Buchanan ascertained that Bishop Polk's nervous sensibility was so acute that, if by accident he touched a piece of brass in the night, when he could not see what he had touched, he immediately felt the influence through his system, and recognised an offensive metallic taste.

The discovery of such sensitiveness in one of the most vigorous men, in mind and body, of his day, led Dr. Buchanan to believe it might be found in many others. It is needless to say his conjecture was correct. Accordingly, in the numerous neurological experiments which he afterwards commenced, he was accustomed to place metals of different kinds in the hands of persons of acute sensibility, for the purpose of ascertaining whether they could feel any peculiar influence, recognise any peculiar taste, or appreciate the difference of metals, by any impression upon their own sensitive nerves. It soon appeared that the power was quite common, and there were a large number of persons who could determine by touching a piece of metal, or by holding it in their hands, what the metal was, as they recognised a peculiar influence proceeding from it, which in a few moments gave them a distinct taste in the mouth. But this sensitiveness was not confined to metallic substances. Every substance possessing a decided taste—sugar, salt, nutmeg, pepper, acid, etc.—appeared to be capable of transferring its influence. The influence appeared to affect the hand, and then travel upwards. He afterwards demonstrated when a galvanic or electric current passed through a medicinal substance, the influence of the substance was transmitted with the current, detected and described by the person operated upon. Medicinal substances, enclosed in paper, were readily recognised and described by their effects. In due time, stranger still, a geological specimen, an article worn, a letter written upon, a photograph which had been handled, a coin, etc., transmitted their influence, and the psychometrist was enabled to read off the history concerning the particular object.

Nearly fifty years have elapsed since the discovery of this "strange new science" and art. "To-day it is widely known, has its respected and competent practitioners, who are able to describe the mental and vital peculiarities of those who visit or write them, and who create astonishment and delight by the fidelity and fulness of the descriptions which they send to persons unknown, and at vast distances. They give minute analysis of character and revelations of particulars *known only to the one described*, pointing out with parental delicacy and tenderness the defects which need correction, or in the perverse and depraved they explain what egotism would deny, but what society, family, and friends recognise to be too true."

PSYCHOMETRIC REFLECTIONS.

Professor J. W. Draper says:—"A shadow never falls upon a wall without leaving thereupon a permanent trace—a trace made visible by resorting to proper processes. Upon the walls of private apartments, where we think the eye of intrusion is altogether shut out, and our retirement can never be profaned, there exists the vestiges of our acts, silhouettes of whatever we have done. It is a crushing thought to whoever has committed secret crime, that the picture of his deed, and the very echo of his words, may be seen and heard countless years after he has gone the way of all flesh, and left a reputation for 'respectability' to his children."

Detectives have received impressions from a scene of crime, a clue to the unravelment of the mystery and the detection of the criminal. Yet they could not trace the impressions to anything they saw or heard during their preliminary investigations. No detective will throw aside such impressions. Indeed, those most successful are those who, while paying attention to all outward and so-called tangible clues, *do not neglect for one moment* the impressions received, and the thoughts *felt*, when gathering information likely to lead to the detection of the law-breakers. Hugh Miller was right when he said, "I suspect that there are provinces in the mind that physicians have not entered into."

Thoughts are things—living, real and tangible, images, visions, deep and pungent sensations—which exist after their creation distinct and apart from ourselves—"Footprints on the sands of time," in more senses than one. We all leave our mark in a thousand subtle ways. No material microscope or telescope can detect, nevertheless our mark can be discovered by the powers of the human soul. From our cradle to the grave—does it stop there? —every thought, emotion, movement, and action have left their subtle traces, so that our whole life can be traced out by the psychometric expert. We verily give hostages to fortune all through life.

PSYCHOMETRIC SENSITIVES.

Professor Denton was very fortunate in having in his wife, children, and in his sister, Mrs. Cridge, gifted psychometers. His sister possessed this psychic, intuitive faculty in a high degree. Dr. Buchanan was equally fortunate; not only was his wife a first-class sensitive, but he discovered the faculty in several university professors, and in students innumerable. Denton in his travels over America, Europe, and Australia found several hundred good sensitives, some of whom have since made a reputation both in Europe and America for their powers.

One important fact we learn from these pioneers in psychometric research is that not one of these persons knew they were endowed with the psychometric gift prior to taking part in classes or experiments.

The possession of the faculty is not confined to any age, or to the gentle sex; and Denton concludes, as an average, that one female in four and one man in ten are psychometric sensitives. The possibility is all healthy, sensitive, refined, intuitive, and impressionable persons possess the soul-measuring faculty, and this faculty, like all other innate human powers, can be cultivated and brought to a high stage of perfection.

The psychometer, unlike the induced clairvoyant or entranced medium, is in general, or outwardly at least, a mere spectator, as one who beholds a drama or witnesses a panorama, and tells in his own way to someone else what he sees and what he thinks about it. The sensitive can dwell on what is seen, examine it closely, and record individual opinions of the impressions of the persons, incidents, and scenes of the long hidden thus brought to light. The sensitive has merely to hold the object in hand—as Mrs. Coates is represented doing in frontispiece—or hold it to the forehead (temple), when he or she is enabled to come in contact with the soul of the person or thing with which the object has been in relation. There is no loss of external consciousness, no "up rush" of the subliminal, obliterating and overlapping that of common life. The sensitive appears to be in a perfectly normal condition during the whole time of examination, can lay the article down, noticing what takes place, and entering into conversation with those in the room, or drawing subjects, seen or not, as they think best.

WHAT PSYCHOMETRY CAN DO.

We can do little more than give a few general illustrations. Professor Denton, having thoroughly satisfied himself of the reality of psychometry, wondered if letters had photographed upon them the impressions of the life and the image of the writer. Why not fossils? "He gave his sister a specimen from the carboniferous formation; closing her eyes, she described those swamps and trees, with their tufted heads and scaly trunks, with the great frog-like animals that existed in that age. To his inexpressible delight the key to the ages was in his hands. He concluded that nature had been photographing from the very first. The black islands that floated upon the fiery sea, the gelatinous dots, the first life on our planet, up through everything that flew or swam, had been photographed by Nature, and ten thousand experiments had confirmed the theory. He got a specimen of the lava that flowed from Kilava, in Hawaii, in 1848. His sister by its means described the boiling ocean, the cataract of molten lava that almost equalled Niagara in size. A small fragment of a meteorite that fell in Painesville, O., was given to his wife's mother, a sensitive who did not then believe in psychometry. This is what she said: 'I seem to be travelling away, away, through nothing, right forward. I see what look like stars and mist. I seem to be taken right up; the other specimens took me down.' His wife, independently, gave a similar description, but saw it revolving, and its tail of sparks. He took steps to prove that this was not mind reading by wrapping the specimens in paper, shaking them up in a hat, and allowing the sensitive to pick out one and describe it, without anyone knowing which it was. Among them were a fragment of brick from ancient Rome, antimony from Borneo, silver from Mexico, basalt from Fingal's Cave. Each place was described correctly by the sensitive in the most minute detail. A fragment from the Mount of Olives brought a description of Jerusalem; and one from the Great Pyramid enabled a young man of Melbourne to name and describe it. There was a practical side to the question. His wife had, from a chip of wood, described a suicide; this was subsequently confirmed. A number of experiments from a fragment of Kent's Cave, fragments from Pompeii and other places brought minute descriptions from the sensitive."

Mr. Stead bears his testimony to psychometry. He gave a shilling to two ladies, at different periods, and unknown to each other. In fact, they were perfect strangers. This shilling, in his mind, had a special story connected with it. The first lady lived in Wimbledon, and had the profession of being a clairvoyante. To use Mr. Stead's own words, he states:—"I took from my purse a shilling which I most prized of all the pieces of money in my possession. I said nothing to her beyond that I had carried it in my pocket for several years. She held the shilling in her hand for sometime, and said: —'This carries me back to a time of confusion and much anxiety, with a feeling that everything depended upon a successful result. This shilling brings me a vision of a very low woman, ignorant and drunken, with whom you had much better have nothing to do. There is a great deal of fever about. I feel great pains, as if I had rheumatic fever in my ankles and joints, but especially in my ankles and my throat. I suffer horribly in my throat; it is an awful pain. And now I feel a coarse, bare hand pass over my brow as distinctly as if you had laid your hand there. It must be her hand. I feel the loss of a child. This woman is brought to me by another. She is about thirty-two years; about five feet high, with dark brown hair, grey eyes, small, nicely-formed nose, large mouth.'" "Can you tell me her name?" asked Mr. Stead. "Not certain, but I think it seems like Annie." "That is all right," said Mr. Stead, and he told her the story of that shilling. About a month afterwards, Mr. Stead tried a Swedish opera singer, who had clairvoyant powers, with the shilling. She pressed it to her brow, and then she told Mr. Stead "she saw a poor woman give him, from her pocket-money, the last shilling she possessed. She has a great admiration for you, she said. She seems to think you have saved her, but she is not *une grande dame*. Indeed, she seems to be a girl of the town." Mr. Stead said:—"I had not spoken a word, or given her the least hint of the story of the shilling." Now, what are the facts? Mr. Stead says that he "was standing his trial at the Old Bailey, a poor outcast girl of the streets, who was dying of a loathsome disease in the hospital, asked that the only shilling that she possessed in the world, might be given to the fund which was being raised in his defence. It was handed to him when he came out of jail, with, 'From a dying girl in hospital, who gives her last shilling,' written on the paper." He (Mr. Stead) has carried it about him ever since, never allowing it to be out of his possession for a single day.

The symptoms which the first clairvoyante, or psychometrix, described, were very like those which this poor creature was suffering from in her dying hours. It is too probable that the donor was a low, drunken woman.

These two readings are actually more psychometric than clairvoyant, because, from the clue furnished, they went back and described the conditions and surroundings of the woman who parted with this shilling. They were not thought-readers, because they did not describe what was passing in Mr. Stead's mind. Mr. Stead's experiences fairly illustrate the exercise, in the earlier stages of employment, of the psychometric faculty.

While engaged writing the "Real Ghost Stories," Mr. Stead says:—"My attention was called to a young lady, Miss Catherine Ross, of 41 High Street, Smethwick, Birmingham, who, being left with an invalid sister to provide for, and without other available profession or industry, bethought herself of a curious gift of reading character, with which she seems to have been born, and had subsequently succeeded in earning a more or less precarious income by writing out characters at the modest fee of 5s. You sent her any article you pleased that had been in contact with the object, and she sent you by return a written analysis of the subject's character. I sent her various articles from one person at different times, not telling her they were from the same person. At one time a tuft of hair from his beard, at another time a fragment of a nail, and a third time a scrap of handwriting. Each delineation of character differed in some points from the other two, but all agreed, and they were all remarkably correct. When she sent the last she added, 'I don't know how it is, but I feel I have described this person before.' I have tried her since then with locks of hair from persons of the most varied disposition, and have found her wonderfully correct."

"All these things are very wonderful, but the cumulative value of the evidence is too great for any one to pooh-pooh it as antecedently impossible. The chances against it being a mere coincidence are many millions to one."

I believe had this young lady, or others thus endowed, had the training, such as Buchanan, Denton, or other experienced teachers give their pupils, she would make a high class psychometer.

Rev. Minot J. Savage had a paper in a recent number of *The Arena*, on Psychical Research, etc., in which he said—"On a certain morning I visited a psychometrist. Several experiments were made. I will relate only one, as a good specimen of what has occurred in my presence more than once. The lady was not entranced or, so far as I could see, in any other than her normal condition. I handed her a letter which I had recently received. She took it, and held it in her right hand, pressing it close, so as to come into as vital contact with it as possible. I had taken it out of its envelope, so that she might touch it more effectively, but it was not unfolded even so much as to give her an opportunity to see even the name. It was written by a man whom she had never seen, and of whom she had never heard. After holding it a moment she said, 'This man is either a minister or a lawyer; I cannot tell which. He is a man of a good deal more than usual intellectual power. And yet he has never met with any success in life as one would have expected, considering his natural ability. Something has happened to thwart him and interfere with his success. At the present time he is suffering with severe illness and mental depression. He has pain here' (putting her hand to the back of her head, at the base of the brain).

"She said much more, describing the man as well as I could have done it myself. But I will quote no more, for I wish to let a few salient points stand in clear outline. These points I will number, for the sake of clearness:—

1. "She tells me he is a man, though she has not even glanced at the letter."

2. "She says he is either a minister or a lawyer; she cannot tell which. No wonder, for he was both; that is, he had preached for some years, then he had left the pulpit, studied law, and at this time was not actively engaged in either profession."

3. "She speaks of his great natural ability. This was true in a most marked degree."

4. "But he had not succeeded as one would have expected. This again was strikingly true. Certain things had happened—which I do not feel at liberty to publish—which had broken off his career in the middle and made his short life seem abortive."

About eighteen years ago a lady in Swansea sent me a lock of hair, and asked me to send her my impressions. I did so, which I remember were not pleasant. I informed her, as near as my recollection now serves, that the person to whom the hair belonged was seriously ill. No earthly skill could do anything for him. Diagnosing the character of the insidious disease which was then undermining a once powerful and active organisation, I felt constrained to add he *would live six weeks*. I held the envelope, with its contents, in my left hand, and wrote the impressions as they came with my right. I remember hesitating about sending that letter, but eventually sent it. The accuracy of my diagnosis, description of the patient, and the fulfilment of the prophecy as to his death were substantiated in a Swansea paper, *The Bat*. The patient was no other than Captain Hudson, the British master mariner who sailed the first ship on teetotal principles from a British port, and who subsequently became one of the most powerful of British mesmerists. The lady who sent the lock of hair was his wife, and the lady who contributed the letter to the papers was his widow. Of similar experiences Mrs. Coates and I have had many.

HOW TO CULTIVATE THE PSYCHOMETRIC FACULTY.

Class Experiments.—The sensitives are not to be magnetised or unduly influenced by positive manner and suggestions, but are to sit in their normal state (and without mental effort or straining to find out what they have in their hands), and simply give expression to their impressions—sensations, tastes, etc., if any, and no matter how strange to them these may be. Let the experimenter or operator place different metallic substances in their hands, taking care that these substances are carefully covered with tissue paper or other light substance, which will help to hide their character, and at the same time not prevent their influence being imparted, or try them with medical substances. In those sufficiently sensitive, an emetic will produce a feeling of nausea. The substance must be put down before it causes vomiting. Geological specimens can be given—a shell, a tooth, or tusk. Let the experimenter record the utterances patiently, and seek confirmation of the description from an examination of the specimen subsequently. He should not know what special specimen it is previous to the psychometer's declared opinion. Good specimens are best. Thus a fragment of pottery, a piece of scori, or a bit of brick from, say, Pompeii would present material from which the psychometrist could glean strong and vivid impressions.

If a medical man is not satisfied as to the correct pathological conditions of his patient, he might ask the psychometer to take some article of the patient in hand, and get, in the sensitive's own—and therefore very likely untechnical—language, what he feels and sees regarding this particular patient's case. Unsuspected abscesses and tumours have been correctly pointed out in this way.

In the same way a correct diagnosis of character can be given in many instances more correctly, more subtle, and penetrating in detail, than estimates built upon mere external and physical signs of temperament and cranial contours.

Lay a coin on a polished surface of steel. Breathe upon it, and all the surface will be affected save the portion on which the coin lay. In a few minutes neither trace of breathing nor of the coin are likely to be seen on the surface of the polished steel. Breathe again, and the hitherto unseen image of the coin is brought to light. In like manner, everything we touch records invisibly to us that action. Hand your sensitive a letter which has been written in love or joy, grief or pungent sorrow, and let them give expression to their sensations. As the breath brought back the image on the steel, so will the nervous and the psychic impressionability of the sensitive bring to light the various emotions which actuated the writers who penned the letters. Mr. G. H. Lewes says "that he has brushed the surface of the polished plate with a camel's-hair brush, yet on breathing upon it the image of the coin previously laid upon it was distinctly visible." The mere casual handling of letters by intermediates will not obliterate the influence of the original writers; they have permeated the paper with their influence, so that, if a score or more of psychometrists held the paper, they would coincide, perhaps not in their language, but in their descriptions of the originals and the state of their minds while writing.

The experimenter may help, by asking a few judicious but not leading questions, to direct and guide the attention of the psychometrist. The description will be a capital delineation of the individual who wrote the letter. We have frequently tested the sincerity of correspondents, real and other friends, by this process. If the results have sometimes been unpleasant revelations, we have yet to find in any case that we have been mistaken. How is the sensitive able to glean so much of the real character of the original? one is inclined to ask. While writing, sincerity and earnestness leave a deeper impression than indifference, pretence, or ordinary come-to-tea politeness. Some letters are instinct with the writer's identity, individuality, masculinity, earnestness, and enthusiasm. Others are lacking in these things, because the writers were devoid of these qualities, while others vary at different times. The writer writes as *his soul* moves him, and the writing expresses his aims and hopes as they appear to his external consciousness. While writing, *his soul* draws his image on the paper, and pictures out thereon his real thoughts; and when the sensitive gets hold of the letter, outstands the image of the writer and the imagery of his thoughts. The psychic consciousness of the psychometer grasps the details and describes them.

"The strange new science of psychometry" is of profound interest to all. Psychometers are to be found in every household. The whole subject is one about which a good deal more could be easily written, but this must do.

Those who desire to understand psychometry cannot do better than read up fully the literature of the subject, and those who desire to practise psychometry may do much to ascertain whether they possess the faculty in any degree; but all are warned to have nothing to do with persons who undertake to *develop* their powers, a *self-evident absurdity*.

CHAPTER V.

THOUGHT-TRANSFERENCE AND TELEPATHY.

THOUGHT-TRANSFERENCE is evidently a phase of psychic perception. In some respects it bears a greater relation to feeling than sight. It is distinguished from pure clairvoyance by the result of experiment. For instance, suppose I had in the Rothesay case designed M. C., the clairvoyante, should see "a maid in the room, dressed in a black dress, with neat white collar and cuffs, wearing a nicely-trimmed white apron, and a white tulle cap with bows and streamers, or that a black-and-white spotted cat lay comfortably coiled up upon the hearth-rug, or some other strongly-projected mental image." Now, suppose while M. C. was examining the room, she declared she *saw* the maid, and described her, or the cat, or other objects projected from my mind, and described these, then this would be a case of thought-transference.

There is a distinction between thought-transference and thought-reading. It is no mere fanciful distinction either. Thought-transference occurs when the ideas, thoughts, and emotions of one mind are projected by intense action and received by the sensitive and impressionable mind of another—awake or asleep is immaterial—so long as it occurs without pre-arrangement and contact.

Telepathy is a more vivid form of sudden and unexpected thought-transference, in which the intense thoughts and wishes of one person, more or less in sympathy, are suddenly transferred to the consciousness of another. The thoughts transmitted are often so intense as to be accompanied by the vision of the person, and by the sound of their voice.

Telepathy bears about the same relation to thought-transference as "second sight" does to clairvoyance. Thought-transference and clairvoyance can be cultivated. Not so telepathy and second sight. They are phenomena, which belong to the unexpected, portents of the unusual, or sudden revelations of what is, and what is about to happen. Doubtless, there are conditions more favourable than others for inception of these. One needs to be "in spirit on the Lord's day," or any day, before telepathic and second sight messages are secured. Hence it is noticed telepathic revelations mostly come in the quietude of the evening, just before sleep, between sleep and waking, and under similar conditions favourable to passivity and receptivity in the sensitive or percipient.

In thought-reading both operator and sensitive are aware that something is to be done, and indications, intentional or otherwise, are given to make the thought-reader find out what is required. More or less sensitiveness is required in both phases. In telepathy and thought-transference the psychic elements are in the ascendency; in thought-reading they may be more or less present, but intention, sensitiveness, and muscular contact are adequate enough, I think, to account for the phenomena, as witnessed at public entertainments—so far, at least, as these entertainments are genuine.

How do we think? what are thoughts? and how are thoughts transferred? are reasonable questions, and merit more elaborate solution than is possible in an elementary work like this.

We think in pictures: words are but vehicles of thought. In thought-transference we can successfully project actions, or a series of actions, by forming in our minds a scene or picture of what is done and what is to be reproduced. When, however, we think of a sentence consisting of few or many words, there is nothing more difficult to convey. Words belong to our external life here, and are but arbitrary expressions and signs for what in the internal or soul-life is flashed telepathically from mind to mind.

Thoughts are things for good or ill, veritable and living realities, apart from our exterior selves, independent of words. The more words, often the less thought. Try to teach a child by the slow, dry-as-dust method of words, and the road to knowledge is hard and wearisome. Convey the same thoughts by illustrations and experiments, and the child's mind at once grasps the ideas we desire to convey.

Thoughts are living entities (how poor are words!) which our own souls have given birth to, or created in the intensity of our love, wisdom, or passion. One Eastern adept has taught, "A good thought is perpetuated as an active, beneficent power, an evil one as a malignant demon. The Hindoo calls this *karma*. The adept evolves these shapes consciously; other men throw them off unconsciously." How true in our experience! The thoughts of some men blast, while those of others bless. There is wisdom in thinking deliberately, intelligently, and therefore conscientiously, not passionately, impulsively, or carelessly.

In thought-transference the reproduction of exact words and dates seems to be most difficult. Indeed, the transmission of arbitrary words and signs is apparently the most difficult. The reason, I conclude, is, ideas belong to our inner, real, and spiritual life, and names, words, and dates to our exterior existence. The ideas can be expressed in the language of the sensitive, according to culture or the want of it. If the true lineaments of the picture are given, need we be too exacting as to the special frame surrounding the picture?

Notwithstanding the difficulty in transference and the reading of the exact words, this has also been frequently done. A very high state of receptivity and sensitiveness, however, is necessary in the percipient.

An incident of exact word-reading is related by Gerald Massey, the distinguished philosopher and poet. Mr. Massey met Mr. Home at the London terminus just on his (Mr. Massey's) arrival from Hertfordshire. Home and he entered into conversation, during which Home suddenly said "he hoped Mr. Massey would go on with his poem."

"What did he mean?" asked Mr. Massey.

"The poem," replied Home, "you composed four lines of just now in the train."

This was surprising to Mr. Massey, who had actually composed, but had not written, the four lines of a new poem on the journey. Mr. Massey challenged Mr. Home to repeat the lines, which Home did word for word.

How are thoughts transferred? No one can positively say. There are theories enough—the *theory of brain-waves* and of *a universal impalpable elastic ether*, of *undulating motions*, or other more or less materialistic hypothesis.[E]

We know there are no psychic phenomena without their corresponding physical correlatives, and, in this life at least, these are in thoughts evolved without producing corresponding molecular changes in the brain.

We notice the human brain is capable of being, and is, acted upon daily by much less subtle influences than mental impressions. We can appreciate light impinged upon our cerebral centres at the rate of millions of undulations, and sound as the result of 20,000 to 30,000 vibrations per second. So sensitives, when in the mesmeric or psychic states, are readily acted upon, and respond as in thought-transference to our thoughts and sensations, and veritably read our minds, because of the *rapport* or sympathy thus established. Whether they become percipients of the nerve-vibrations which escape from our own sensoriums or not, what does it matter *if they can, as they frequently do*, read our minds?

"Professor Wheaton," says Hudson Tuttle, "devised a means of illustrating sympathy. If a sounding board is placed so as to resound to all instruments of the orchestra, and connected by a metallic rod of considerable length with the sounding board of a harp or piano, the instrument will accurately repeat the notes transmitted.

"The nervous system, in its two-fold relation to the physical and spiritual being, is inconceivably more finely organised than the most perfect musical instrument, and is possessed of finer sensitiveness.

"It must not be inferred that all minds are equally receptive. Light falls on all substances alike, but is very differently affected by each substance. One class of bodies absorb all but the yellow rays, another all but the blue, another all but the red, because these substances are so organised that they respond only to the waves of the colours reflected."

All persons do not hear alike. They receive certain sounds and are deaf to all others, although the sound-waves strike all tympanums alike. All persons do not see alike. Some perceive colours, others cannot distinguish between one colour and another, or can only see the more striking colours—fineness of shade they do not perceive. So there are individuals who cannot receive mental impressions, unless, indeed, they are conveyed in the baldest and most esoteric manner. In a word to convey and receive impressions they must be sent along the line of the least resistance, that of *true sympathy*. There must be one mind adequate to the projection, and another mind sufficiently sensitive to receive and record the thoughts projected.

TRANSFERENCE OF TASTE IN THE MESMERIC STATE.

The operator will slowly eat or taste half-a-dozen lozenges or sweets of different flavours, and the subject or sensitive most in sympathy with him will also in imagination eat of and describe the taste of the various sweets, concerning which he has no other knowledge than the thoughts of eating and tasting, which are transmitted to him from the brain of the operator. The mere eating of the lozenges by the operator, without his being fully aware of the fact, will deepen the impression on the operator's mind, and help to concentrate his energies for the transmission of his ideas or mental suggestions to his subject.

A step or two further and we find with greater sensitiveness the sensitives can read the thoughts of the operator, whether the thoughts were transmitted intentionally or not.

"We are compelled (says Dr. Hands) to acknowledge that certain emanating undulations from the sensorium can generate different series of thoughts, and that the trembling organisation, or parts of it, can, by flinging or throwing off distinct or particular pulsatory waves, inoculate or produce like vibrations in another person's brain, making up in it identical thoughts, followed by like feelings, and often in this way, perhaps, capable of inciting, *through sympathy*, like enactments of deeds and pursuits."

THOUGHT-TRANSFERENCE IN DREAMS.

The following interesting letter appeared in *The Phrenological Magazine* (p. 260, April, 1890), and as I know of the *bona-fides* of the writer, I have much pleasure in reproducing it:—

"DEAR SIR,—This morning, at a little before four o'clock, I awoke as the outcome of great mental distress and grief through which I had just passed in a dream, my body trembling and in a cold perspiration. I had been walking with my little boy, aged five and a half years, and some friends. A heavy rain overtaking us, we stood up for shelter; and venturing forth into a maze of streets, I missed my two friends, who, threading among the people, had turned into a side street without my noticing. Looking for them, my boy slipped from me, and was lost in the crowd. I became bewildered by the strange labyrinth of streets and turnings, and quickly taking one of them which gave an elevated position, I looked down on the many windings, but could nowhere see my boy. It was to me an unknown locality, and, running down among the people, I was soon sobbing aloud in my distress, and calling out the name of the child, when I awoke. With wakefulness came a sense of relief and thankfulness. Gladly realising that the whole was only a dream, and still scarcely awake, I was startled by a cry of terror and pain from an adjoining bedroom—such a cry as could not be left unheeded. It came from the same child, and pierced me with a distinct sense of pain. I was immediately by his side. My voice calmed him. 'I thought I was lost' was all he could say, and doubtless he was soon composed and asleep again. To me the coincidence was too remarkable and without parallel in my own experience. Later on, at breakfast, the child gave further his dream that he *had been out with me and was lost*. I am only familiar with such things in my reading. Mr. Coates's article in last month's *Phrenological Magazine* (page 143) mentions that, 'when the Prince Imperial died from assegai thrusts in Zululand, his mother in England felt the intensity of his thoughts at the time, felt the savage lance pierce her own side, and knew or felt at the time that she was childless.' But I am not of the *spirituelle* type, with only a thin parchment separation between this life of realities and the great beyond, of those who, privileged to live in close touch with the future, are the subjects of premonitions and warnings. My spirituality 4 to 5 and reflectives 6 point rather the other way, but I shall, nevertheless, hold tight to the lad. What is the underlying cause of the coincidence? Which of the two minds influenced the other, if either?—Yours truly,

"G. Cox.

"16 Bramfield Road,
Wandsworth Common, April 20, 1890."

In this case of thought-transference, I am inclined to the opinion that the father's mind influenced that of the boy, the son being the more sensitive of the two. Mr. Cox dreamt an ordinary but pretty vivid dream, which aroused from its nature vivid and intense anxiety on his part. A similar train of thought was awakened in the child. If thought-transference occurs in waking life, why not in sleep, when, as abundant telepathic instances testify, the phenomenon is of most frequent occurrence.

THOUGHT-TRANSFERENCE AT SEA.

The percipient was Captain G. A. Johnson, of the schooner "Augusta H. Johnson." He had sailed from Quero for home. On the voyage he encountered a terrible hurricane. On the second day he saw a disabled brig, and near by a barque. He was anxious to reach home, and, thinking the barque would assist the brig, continued on.

But the impression came that he must turn back and board the brig. He could not shake it off, and at last he, with four men, boarded the brig in a dory. He found her deserted, and made sail in her. After a time they saw an object ahead, appearing like a man on a cake of ice. The dory was again manned, and set to the rescue. It proved to be the mate of the barque "Leawood" clinging to the bottom of an overturned boat, which, being white, appeared in the distance as ice.

The captain's sensitiveness may have been aroused by the exhaustion of so much wakefulness and care during the length of the storm, the sight of the derelict and deserted brig; at the same time the premonitions were opposed to his own desire and anxiety to get home.

THOUGHT-TRANSFERENCE FROM THE DYING TO THE LIVING IN DREAM.

The following, by E. Ede, M.D., of Guilford (J.S.P.R., July, 1882):—

"Lady G. and her sister had been spending the evening with their mother, who was in her usual health and spirits when they left her. In the middle of the night the sister awoke in a fright, and said to her husband, 'I must go to my mother at once; do order the carriage. I am sure she is ill.' The husband, after trying in vain to convince his wife that it was only a fancy, ordered the carriage. As she was approaching the house, where two roads met, she saw lady G.'s carriage. When they met, each asked the other why she was there. The same reply was made by both—'I could not sleep, feeling sure my mother was ill, and so I came to see.' As they came in sight, they saw their mother's confidential maid at the door, who told them when they arrived that their mother had taken suddenly ill, and was dying, and had expressed an earnest wish to see her daughters."

The percipients having been so lately in company and sympathy with their mother possibly rendered them more susceptible to her influence.

THOUGHT-TRANSFERENCE FROM THE DEAD (?) TO THE LIVING IN DREAM.

Related by Mr. Myers, page 208, Proceedings S.P.R., July, 1892:—

"About March, 1857, Mrs. Mennier, in England, dreamt that she saw her brother, whose whereabouts she did not know, standing headless at the foot of the bed with his head lying in a coffin by his side. The dream was at once mentioned. It afterwards appeared that at about the time the head of the brother seen, Mr. Wellington, was actually cut off by the Chinese at Sarawak." On this case, Mr. Gurney remarks—"This dream, if it is to be telepathically explained, must apparently have been due to the last flash of thought in the brother's consciousness. It may seem strange that a definite picture of his mode of death should present itself to a man in the instant of receiving an unexpected and fatal blow; but, as Hobbes said, 'Thought is quick.' The coffin, at any rate, may be taken as an item of death-imagery supplied by the dreamer's mind."

"We have now, however," says Mr. Myers, "seen a letter from Sir James Brookes (Rajah of Sarawak), and an extract from the *Straits Times* of March 21st, 1857, in the (London) *Times* for April 29th, 1857, which makes it, I think, quite conceivable that the dream was a reflection of knowledge acquired after death, and the head on the coffin had a distinct meaning." Sir James Brookes says:—"Poor Wellington's remains were consumed [by the Chinese]; his head, borne off in triumph, alone attesting his previous murder." The *Straits Times* says:—"The head was given up on the following day. The head, therefore, and the head alone, must have been buried by Mr. Wellington's friends; and its appearance in the dream *on the coffin*, with a headless body standing beside it, is a coincidence even more significant than the facts which Mr. Gurney had before him when he wrote."

The transmission of thought from a spirit discarnate to one incarnate, whose body was asleep, should not be esteemed impossible. Abundant instances, equally well substantiated, might be recorded did space permit.

THOUGHT TRANSFERENCE IN PRAYER.

This may be a common experience, but only once in my life have I had conscious knowledge of anything so remarkable. For some years before devoting my attention to these subjects, I resided in Liverpool, and had been a member of the Zion Methodist Church, or Chapel, in Everton, and in time was duly placed on the local preachers' plan. In this capacity I became acquainted with a worthy old man—a chapel-keeper, who looked after the meeting house situated in —— street. He had been an old soldier, and possessed something of the faith of the Roman centurion. Poor in the things of this world, he was rich in the sublimity of his love to God and the nobility and purity of his life. I never think of "Old Daddy Walker" but his character and this incident comes to my mind, viz.:—One morning I was hurrying down West Derby Road to business, and, indeed had got halfway down Brunswick Road, when I commenced to think about old Walker (I had not seen or thought of him for some months). I attempted to throw aside my impressions, as passing thoughts. No use. I became worried about him, and was asking myself questions. "Was he ill?" "Maybe, he is in want?" "I think I will hurry back and see?" I had not much time to spare. It would consume fully twenty minutes to walk back. After hesitating, I went up Brunswick Road and up West Derby Road, and to —— Street, and tapped at the door of his house. There was no response. The street door was slightly ajar. I went in, and found the old pair on their knees in the kitchen. He was engaged in earnest prayer. After kindly salutations, I apologised for intruding, and told him, as I went to business, "I had been bothered about him in my mind, and did not feel satisfied until I had seen him, and knew the truth." He told me, as near as I can recollect, "He was at his last extremity. There was no food or fuel in the house, he had no money, and he had been putting the whole case before the Lord." I had half a sovereign about me, which I had taken out of the house for an entirely different purpose. This I gave to him. The old man, rubbing a tear from his eye, looking at his wife, said: "Mary, don't thee doubt the Lord anymore. I said He would help, and He has given me what I asked for." Old Walker went on to explain, not only his bad fix, but that he had no money to buy firewood with. He meant that he bought up old wood and tar-barrels, which he cut up into lengths and made into bundles, and sold for firewood; and that he had asked the Lord for ten shillings, as he wanted that sum to buy a certain lot which could be obtained for that amount. The old man obtained what he asked for. He believed the Lord had answered his prayer.

THOUGHT TRANSMISSION IN PRAYER.

Since writing the above, the following came under my notice. In the J.S.P.R., May, 1885, Dr. Joseph Smith, Warrington, England, says:—

"I was sitting one evening reading, when a voice came to me, saying: 'Send a loaf to James Grady's.' I continued reading, and the voice continued with greater emphasis, and this time it was accompanied with an irresistible impulse to get up. I obeyed, and went into the village and bought a loaf of bread, and, seeing a lad at the shop door, I asked him if he knew James Grady. He said he did, so I bade him carry it and say a gentleman sent it. Mrs. Grady was a member of my class, and I went next morning to see what came of it, when she told me a strange thing happened to her last night. She said she wished to put the children to bed, they began to cry for want of food, and she had nothing to give them. She then went to prayer, to ask God to give them something. Soon after which the lad came to the door with the loaf. I calculated, on inquiry, that the prayer and the voice I heard exactly coincided in point of time."

"More things are wrought by prayer
Than this world dreams of."

Those who know anything of Methodism, will know this. The Methodists have a profound faith in prayer, and also there is a very close relationship between a class-leader and his members. Dr. Smith was, therefore, all the more likely to be the percipient of the woman's earnest and intense prayer to God to feed her hungry children. The Infinite must have an infinite variety of ways of fulfilling His own purposes. Is it unreasonable to suppose that prayer to Him may not be answered indirectly "through means"? and that thought-transference, as in this instance, may be one of the means? If not, why not?

Charitable institutions are maintained; orphans saved, reared, and educated; missions of mercy organised, and the necessary means found by the agency of prayer. Beside "the angels," in That Sphere just beyond the ken of the physical, may not our waves of thought, projected by prayer, be impinged upon, and directly affect susceptible minds in this world, by directing their attention to those works of faith and goodness? Prayer is the language of love, and the outcome of true helplessness and need. A praying man is an earnest man. In prayer thoughts are things—bread upon the waters.

THOUGHT TRANSFERENCE IN DISTRESS.

I withhold the names for family reasons. Mr. —— had been in business in Glasgow for nearly thirty years, and, from comparatively small beginnings, had been very successful. Latterly, he and his family resided in ——, a suburb of Glasgow. Both in the city and in this district Mr. —— was very much respected, being a church member and holding office in —— Free Church. For some time Mr. —— had been ailing, and his medical attendant advised him to take a sea voyage—a thorough change, etc. In compliance with this advice, he took a trip up the Mediterranean. Miss ——, a distant relative of his, had been visiting Glasgow, and, being on terms of intimacy with the family, knew of his departure from Glasgow. About two weeks after he left, she also left Glasgow for Edinburgh. While in the train for Edinburgh, she was overcome with great anxiety for Mrs. ——, his wife. Unable to shake the feeling off, instead of going to Edinburgh, she actually got out of the train halfway, at Falkirk, and took the next train back to Glasgow, and went to her friend's house, whom she found in great distress. Mrs. —— had, about the time Miss —— became distressed in the train, received word that her husband was found dead (having committed suicide) in his berth on the steamer at Constantinople. The state of mind of the newly-made widow re-acted on that of Miss ——. As Miss —— was not only a dear friend, but was noted for her earnest piety, the widow at once earnestly desired to see her. When last these two friends saw each other, everything seemed to contribute to happiness and comfort. Mrs. —— was looking forward hopefully for the return of her husband, restored in health, to herself and children.

THOUGHT TRANSFERENCE IN ORDINARY EXPERIENCE.

Whether thought-transference is a "relic of a decaying faculty," or the "germ of a new and fruitful sense," daily experience in the lives of most furnish abundant evidence of the existence of such a power. My own life has supplied me with abundant evidence of the fact. It is a common occurrence with us for either my wife or I to utter or give expression to the thoughts which, for the time being, occupied the conscious plane in the other. It is possible there may have been, as there has been in some instances, some half phrase uttered or manner shown, which in the one have aroused the thoughts expressed by the other.

It has been our habit for several years to stay at Rothesay during the summer season. As an instance of thought-transference quite common in our experience;—On Saturday, 1st October, 1892, I went to the Revision Court at the Town Hall to hear registration disputes settled between Tory and Gladstonian lawyers. Finding nothing to interest me, I entered into conversation with Mr. Thompson, jeweller and hardware merchant, whom I met in the Court, and went with him to his shop in Montague Street, Rothesay. Standing at his door a short time, I noticed a solitary pair of shamrock earrings, composed of crystal brilliants and gold, lying on a tray, with a number of other earrings, in one of the windows. I inquired the price, as I felt sure Mrs. Coates would be pleased with them. They were packed up in a neat box, and I took them home. At dinner, I gave the box to my wife, who said, "What is this, papa?"

"Open and see," I replied.

Animated with a little curiosity, she did, and, as soon as she saw the earrings, said, "Thompson's! Well, papa, that is funny. James (my little son) and I stood at Thompson's window last night, and I admired these earrings. I thought them so neat, and that they would match my brooch. I thought I would like to have them, and then I thought to myself, no; I will not spend the money. I pointed them out to James, and said to him, I am sure if papa saw them, he would buy them—and here you have brought them home. I cannot tell you how much I prize them."

My little boy said, "Thought-reading again, papa!" and, with a good laugh, we proceeded to discuss our dinner. Mrs. Coates had not been in the habit of seeing this particular window, and I am not in the habit of buying jewellery.

I record this trifle here, as one of our common experiences, and I am satisfied similar experiences are common to all.

Another experience is the anticipation of letters and their contents. This is most frequent in the morning, just before rising. I frequently see the letters and the shape of the envelope and style of address before I actually see the letters on my consulting table.

The most common experience of all is recognised by the adage, "Think of the Devil, and he will appear." I have noted this in particular. Sitting at the table, there is "popped" into my mind a thought of someone. I will remark, "I think Mr. or Mrs. —— will be here to-day," and they come. Certainly, all who have come in this way have been relatives or friends; and although they appear subsequent to the thought of them, the evidence in favour of thought-transference may not be esteemed conclusive. I say it is a common experience. I don't think we should despise any experience, because it is common. To be common, indicates there is a basis, amounting to a psychic law, to account for its existence.

Another common experience is the crossing of letters. One person suddenly recollects "So-and-so;" and writes them a letter excusing delay in writing, retailing news, and in all probability writing on some subject more particularly than on others. Strange to say, the person you have written to, has also been engaged writing to you about the same time and on similar subjects. Both have possibly posted their letters at such a time that the delivery has been crossed. I do not say this proves anything; yet I cannot help thinking the experience is too frequent to be accounted for by the usual explanation of accident or coincidence.

Mark Twain's article on "Mental Telegraphy" is fresh in the minds of most magazine readers. Whether that article had a basis in the writer's actual experience or not, it is a pretty common experience with most literary men.

"Distance," says Mr. Tuttle, "has inappreciable influence on the transference of thought. It may take place in the same room, or where the two persons are thousands of miles apart. As a personal experience, I will relate one of many similar incidents which have awakened my attention to this wonderful phenomenon. Sitting by my desk one evening, suddenly as a flash of light, the thought came to write an article for the *Harbinger of Light*, published at Melbourne, Australia. I had, by correspondence, become acquainted with the editor, W. H. Terry, but there had been no letters passed for many a year. I had not thought of him or his journal for I do not know how long a time, and I was amused at first with the idea of writing on the subject suggested. But the impression was so strong that I prepared and forwarded an article. Nearly two months passed before I received a letter from Mr. Terry, requesting me to write an article on the subject on which I have written; and, making due allowance for time, the date of our letters were the same. In our experience, this crossing of letters answering each other has twice occurred—the second by Mr. Terry answering a request of mine."

Dr. Charles W. Hidden, of Newburyport, Mass., U.S.A., reports a somewhat similar experience to that of Mark Twain and the above, which was reported in a recent number of the *Religio-Philosophical Journal*: A very peculiar plot impressed itself upon his mind, and he immediately based a story upon the plot. He read the story to his family, and was about to send it to a publication to which his wife had recently become a subscriber. When the next number arrived he opened it to learn how to forward his manuscript, and great was his surprise to find on the first page a story bearing the title of his own, and a plot almost identical with that which he had written. Parts of the published article appeared word for word. It is needless to add that Dr. Hidden tossed his manuscript into his desk, and it is there yet. His explanation is, that he caught the title and the plot from another, just as Mark Twain caught the plot of the "Big Bonanza" from his friend Simmons.

It would be nigh impossible to illustrate the various phases of thought-transference, ranging, as they do, from the association of ideas which may be aroused by a hint, a half-uttered word, or a gesture, to the unmistakable facts of pure mental transference, and, higher still, to the region of pure psychism, where spirit influences inspire and direct spirit, and thought-bodies are no longer recognised as mere subjective spirits but living and tangible objective personalities, albeit discarnate.

We can say truly with Voltaire, "There is a power that acts within us, without consulting us."

CHAPTER VI.

Thought-Reading Experiments.

Having satisfactory evidence of the reality of thought-transference, it would be interesting to know if this power or faculty can be cultivated, and if so, how? I propose in this chapter to show how this can be done, and how to give thought-reading entertainments.

Experimental mind-reading may be distinguished, for the sake of study, as the abnormal, the normal, and the spurious.

The abnormal, that which takes place in trance, dream, vision, or which may be the product of artificial somnambulism or of some super-sensitive condition of the nervous system, through disease. We observe thought-transference in these conditions, rather than attempt to cultivate it.

The normal, where the phenomena takes place in the ordinary waking state, *without muscular contact*.

The spurious mind-reading, so-called, as the result of musculation or *contact*, but which is, in fact, only muscle-reading.

In both the abnormal and normal, direct transference of thought from mind to mind can only take place when there is the necessary development of psychic activity in the agent or operator, and the equally necessary sensitiveness in the sensitive or percipient.

Classed under muscle-reading are those performances and games in which the sensitive reads not the mind, but some special desire (of those with whom he or she may be placed *in contact*), by a "careful study of the indications unconsciously given by the agent or operator to the percipient or reader."

In both abnormal and normal thought-reading, then, are presented innumerable instances of the possession of psychic faculties; in the muscle-reading phase there may be, and it is possible all successful "readers" have, more or less sensitiveness, to take impressions.

To cultivate mind-reading in a sensitive, the operator should first cultivate in himself the habit of projecting mental pictures, and think of things as seen by the eye, rather than as described by words. This is best done by calling to mind a landscape or domestic scene, by conceiving and mentally building up the same, and, by degrees, getting each feature or detail well stamped in his mind.

It is well in the beginning of these experiments to make the scene as simple, and yet as natural and as complete in detail, as possible. For instance, let the operator think of such a picture as this:—A bright little landscape, having a well-defined cottage on the left, just on the margin of a small lake; boat with two figures in the foreground; rising bank upon the right; and a little higher up a defined windmill, well thrown out by the perspective of blue-ridged and undulating mountains, and sky in the background.

The agent, having satisfied himself of his sensitive's whole or partial powers of psychic perception, might ask:—"Do you see anything now?" and quickly and deliberately go to work, meanwhile formulating definitely such a picture as the above; even allowing himself to get into ecstacies over the scene—peopling the cottage and the mill, and introducing imaginary conversation between the individual dwellers therein, and so on. The sensitive will describe the whole as the same is *felt* or perceived. This experiment may appear to some to be impossible, but the word impossible belongs to the limitations of sense, and not to the range of the things possible to the human spirit.

Some sensitives and mediums take impressions from their surroundings—their clairvoyant revelations are often nothing more than so much Mind-reading. *Nothing more*; but this nothing more is a great deal. Certainly, it may not prove the existence of spirit, apart from the sensitive's own powers; but it does prove that man has other avenues of knowledge than those with which he is usually credited.

The development of mind-reading in the psychic states may be encouraged by a little judicious assistance or direction. Invite the sensitive to pay attention to So-and-so; to visit places, to examine rooms, or describe people whom the sensitive has never seen. But the places, the rooms, and the persons must be *distinctly in the minds* of those persons, or agents, with whom he or she is placed in *rapport*.

During these experiments the sensitive will say, "I *see* this," or describe that other, as if he actually saw. Hence the infinitely close relationship of mind-reading to clairvoyance. Thought-reading in spiritualism will be referred to in the next chapter.

Once possessing a good sensitive, the development of the power, as a matter of fact, lies particularly in the operator's ability to concentrate and focus his thoughts—to think clearly, calmly, vividly, and distinctly himself —and to deliberately and conscientiously project the same.

THE NORMAL EXPERIMENTS WITHOUT CONTACT.

A pleasant hour or so can be profitably filled up on a long winter's evening with experiments in mind reading, without resorting to mesmerism. It will be found that there are mind-readers in every family—some boy, girl, or young woman more sensitive than the rest to impressions.

Sometimes it has been found, when two or more persons think of the same object, as in the "willing game," the impression becomes more vivid, and the sensitive finds, or describes, the article, or thing, more easily. It has been left to the versatility of Professor Lodge, of the University College, Liverpool, to project two distinct images at the same time to a sensitive. He requested two friends to look at a paper that he had given to each. On one paper a square was drawn, and on the other an oblique cross. Neither person knew what the other was looking at, and after they had looked intently at these diagrams for a short time, the sensitive, who was in a normal condition, but blindfold, said:—"I see two figures—first I see one, and then, below that, another. I do not know which I am to draw. I cannot see either plainly." Having been requested to draw what she saw, she drew a square, with an oblique cross inside of it. On being questioned, she replied that she did not know why she placed the cross in the square. The two images projected by distinct minds, intermingled, and were produced, as narrated by Professor Lodge. We can readily see that confusion will arise where a number of persons are thinking of different subjects, or when some positive-minded individual declares mind-reading to be an impossibility.

Something after the above experiments of Professor Lodge are those which were conducted by Mr. Guthrie, a London barrister, and reported by him to the Society of Psychical Research.

A number of diagrams, roughly drawn off-hand at the time, were shown to the agent or precipitant, Mr. G., the subject, or percipient, a lady, being blind-fold. During the process of transference, the agent looked steadily and in silence at the drawing, the subject meanwhile sitting opposite to him, and behind the stand on which the drawing lay, so that it was entirely out of her range of vision had her eyes not been blind-folded.

The agent stopped looking at the drawing when the subject professed herself ready to make the attempt to reproduce it. The time occupied thus was from half a minute to two or three minutes. Then the handkerchief was removed, and she drew with a pencil what had occurred to her mind.

RESULTS OF EXPERIMENTS IN THOUGHT-TRANSFERENCE.

RESULTS OF EXPERIMENTS IN THOUGHT-TRANSFERENCE.

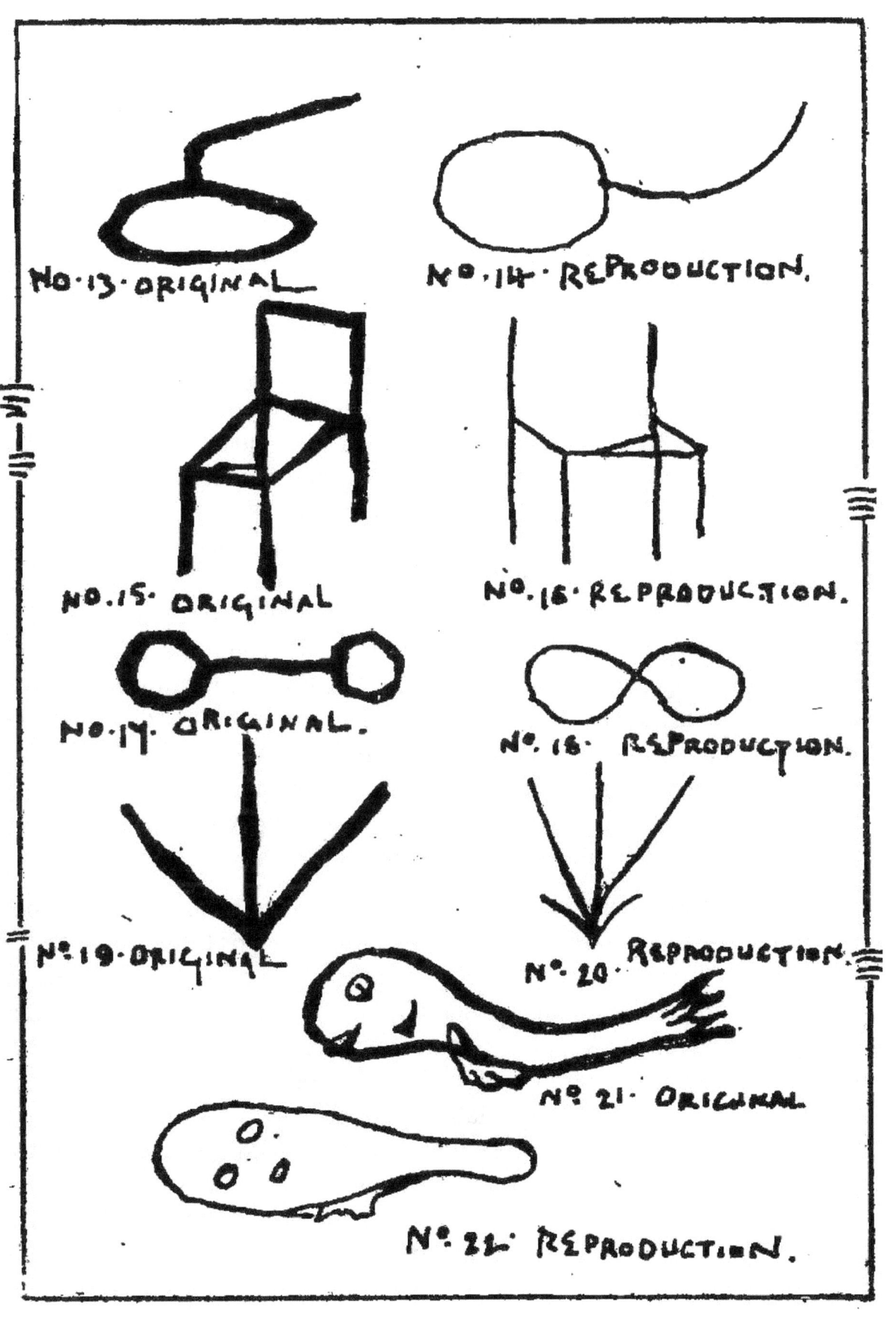

The reproductions were made generally without the agent following or watching the process. We reproduce several of the attempts here, giving both the successes and the failures. Even the failures show the effect Mr. G. produced upon the reader's mind.

The experiments conducted so successfully in the family of the Rev. Mr. Creery, of Boston, and made public by Professor Barrett in *The Journal of Psychical Research*, show to what extent thought-reading may be successfully carried on in the quietude and confidence of a well-regulated family.

The mode of procedure adopted by Professor Barrett to test the faculty as possessed by the children was as follows:—"One of the children," says Professor Barrett, "was sent into an adjoining room, the door of which I saw was closed. On returning to the sitting-room, and closing the door also, I thought upon some object in the house, fixed upon at random. Writing the name down, I showed it to the family present, the strictest silence being preserved throughout. We then all silently thought of the name of the thing selected. In a few seconds the door of the adjoining room was heard to open, and after a short interval the child would enter the sitting-room, generally speaking, with the object selected. No one was allowed to leave the sitting-room after the object had been fixed upon, and no communication with the child was conceivable, as her place was often changed. Further, the only instructions given to the child were to fetch some objects in the house that I would think upon and, together with the family, silently keep in mind, to the exclusion as far as possible of all other ideas."

Now, if Professor Barrett had told the children to select a word, and upon coming into the room were to spell or state what the word was, I question if the experiments would have been so successful. The articles thought of, whether a hair brush, an orange, wine glass, apple, or a playing card, were of such a nature that a definite picture or image of the thing thought of could be formed in the mind. The father, mother, and even Professor Barrett, seem to have been especially in *rapport* with the little sensitives, and thus all the more readily were they able to transmit the mental picture of the articles selected. Trick or collusion in this case is absolutely out of the question. It would be interesting to know if these young sensitives, who were so bright in 1881, still retain, or have increased or lost, their powers.

There were 312 trials made during Professor Barrett's stay of six days, who adds—"One most striking piece of success, when the things selected were divulged to none of the family, was five cards running named correctly on the first trial—the odds against this happening once in our series, being considerably over one million to one. We had altogether a good many similar batches, the two longest runs being eight consecutive successes, once with cards and once with names, when the adverse odds in the former case were over one hundred and forty-two millions to one, and on the latter, something incalculably greater. *Walls and closed doors made no difference.*" [The italics are mine.—J.C.]

Something after the foregoing style are drawing-room entertainments given. If failure result, no one is blamed, and ridiculous mistakes only lend pleasure to the company, where all are known one to the other.

The usual method is to select someone for thought-reader. Lady or gentleman, matters little. He or she is sent out of the room. Some one in the room generally takes the lead, who may suggest the article to be selected and hidden, which the thought-reader is to find. The article selected is thought of by the entire company. The reader is to go to the place where it is, lift it, put it down, or give it to some one else; or to find a certain book and remove it from its place on table or elsewhere, and put it somewhere else; to come in and sit on a certain chair or to lead someone else to it, or perform whatever other test that is decided upon. The reader is admitted into the room, and, if at all receptive, will do or say something like what is desired—often going direct to the spot, lifting the article, or doing the things which the company have decided upon.

A good plan is to get the assistance of one or two friends, use a bag of counters, upon which numbers 10 to 100 are placed; also a smaller bag with numbers 1 to 9. Let the sensitive sit at a table in such a position, so as, if not blindfolded, he or she could not see what the agent has in his hand. Use the small bag to begin with. Let one friend hold the bag, another select a number. When both have carefully looked at it, let it be handed to the agent, who shall fix his eyes steadily upon the figure, and picture the said figure on his mind. The sensitive will in one or two minutes either say or write down what the figure is. If these experiments become satisfactory, the larger bag can be used. The experiments with numbers must not be continued too long, and so weary the faculty. In the same way a number of simple outline designs can be used—these presented one by one to the agent or operator—a fish, a boy and barrow, a fireman with escape, a negro and banjo, a lecturer on platform, an orange, a book, etc., such as are found in children's school books; repeating the same processes as above. No one must speak but the agent and the percipient, nor is the agent to know what the numbers or designs are before the experiments are commenced.

Should failure occur, select another medium. In a company of twenty to thirty persons it will be very strange if a good thought-reading sensitive is not found. In which case, more serious experiments may be attempted subsequently, and attain scientific value.

The thought-reader should be blindfolded, and *resign* himself to the *influence* of the agent or operator. Although he understands that something is expected of him, he is not to be anxious about what, but simply *act* as he *feels* himself prompted.

In proportion as the sensitive is able to give up anxiety and desire, so will he be able to become a good reader.

The operator, or agent, must concentrate his mind upon what is required, and *will* the sensitive to do it. When two or more persons, or all in the room, *are* concentrating their minds upon the thing, object, or word, the sensitive may all the sooner be influenced; but I prefer that one person should be chosen as the operator, and all intended experiments be submitted to him.

The process is analogous to that of mesmerism. We see traces here of the influence of mind over mind. We see the operator determines and the subject performs, although it may not be very clear how thought is actually projected, or in what way it is received, other than already suggested.

Practice makes perfect in this as in other things. Success is proportionate to success. A reader showing a degree of susceptibility at first attempts will generally improve by subsequent efforts. In a similar way, operators will make headway with practice. Some operators and sensitives will be successful at first trial; others again have failed after repeated attempts.

Plenty of time should be taken for all first attempts. Let the operator, for instance, keep his mind thoroughly fixed on the object. Should the reader be going away from it, let the agent strongly wish him to go back, *touch* it, lift it, etc., as previously decided upon by the company.

All sensitive persons are likely to make good thought-readers; the less sensitive, muscle-readers.

MUSCLE-READING ENTERTAINMENTS.

Thought-transference, like clairvoyance, is unequal in power and manifestation, even with good percipients, and cannot be turned on like, and with, the evening gas, to enlighten and entertain. Hence those enterprising entertainers, like Bishop and Cumberland, depended on "muscle-reading," and "backed-up their show" with tricks, some of them so puerile and barefaced that a third-rate conjuror would be ashamed of them.

The general public, however, enjoyed these entertainments. They were something new, and, like "angel's visits," were few and far between. Not only so, but that wonderful combination, the general public, saw that these entertainments were patronised by men of science, such as Carpenter, Beard, Hammond, Baron Kelvin, and others deeply in love with strictly materialistic hypothesis. They were also patronised by "society." These entertainers undertook to read thoughts and expose spiritualism; and as the dear public loves mystery, it went. But the dear public don't like to be "taken in," hence these performances are generally repeated—in the next town.

The following, reported from St. John's, N.B., January 17, 1887, in the *Herald*, is a good illustration of the psychic and muscular indications involved in an experiment of this kind:—"In a 'mind-reading' performance on Saturday night, after several examples indoors, the 'reader,' a young man who belongs to this city, asked for an outdoor test. The party separated, one remaining with the reader, and hid a pin in the side of a little house used by the switchman of the New Brunswick Railway at Mill Street. In their travels they went over the new railway trestle, a most difficult journey. The reader was blindfolded, and one took his wrist, but at the trestle hesitated, fearing to venture, and was told by the reader to let go his wrist and place his hand on his head. The subject did so, and the reader went upon the trestle. Some of the party suggested that the bandage should be removed, but he told them not to mind, and, the subject again taking the wrist, he went over the ice and snow-covered sleepers. With a firm step he crossed to the long wharf, went over as far as the mill gates, then quickly turned, retraced his steps, and went back to the corner of Mill Street. Here he rested a minute, then again took the subject's hand, and in less than five minutes afterwards found the pin. At the conclusion of the test, the reader inquired what the matter had been when they first reached the trestle. It was easily explained. The storm had covered the sleepers with snow, and it was thought dangerous, even for a man not blindfolded to cross them. The subject felt anxious for the reader's safety, and hesitated about going across. The tests were most satisfactory." Thought or mind-reading applied to these experiments is a misnomer. If this young gentleman could "read thoughts" by musculation, or *contact,* he would have known what the matter had been when they first reached the trestle. Muscle-reading is not thought-reading. Hence it is classified as spurious.

Any number of illustrations could be given of such entertainments. The foregoing is sufficiently adequate to give an idea of how these muscle (not thought) reading entertainments are given.

For drawing-room entertainments, first blindfold the reader, who is conducted out of the room while the experiments are decided upon. The blindfolding helps to mystify friends, who think the work is rendered more difficult. As a matter of fact, the reader's work is rendered much more easy. It helps to isolate him, and leaves his mind much less entrammelled by sights and impressions which would otherwise prevent him receiving *the* impressions which it is desirable he should receive.

Suppose the reader is to locate the seat of an imaginary pain, the assistant or operator *pro tem.* will grasp[F] with his left hand the sensitive's right wrist and hold it firmly. While the reader is endeavouring to locate the pain, the operator must give up his will, and think intently on the situation of the pain. The reader will then locate it.

There is less secret in this than appears at first sight. The sensitive, or reader, is simply guided or led by the operator, and the reader's hand either stops partially over or is pressed upon the seat of the pain. He then declares he has found the seat of the pain, and points it out accordingly.

A somewhat similar method is adopted in finding the pin, or the *hole* in which a pin *had been*. The racing and flying about of public thought-readers are only so much "theatrical side," thrown in to give dramatic effect to their performances.

In reading the numbers on bank-notes, or spelling out certain words, a board with the numerals and the alphabet (see front cover) is placed in sight of the audience. The reader takes the wrist of the operator, and, commencing at the left side of the board, proceeds from figure to figure till he detects the right one. The operator thinks only of *one* figure or letter at a time. This is the whole secret of "musculation." Even when the operators are sincere, and are careful to give no conscious indications to the reader, yet it is almost certain, if they keep their mind fixed on the desired figure or letter, object or place, they will unconsciously indicate to the reader the right number or letter.

To find an article, number, or do a certain act, it is necessary for the reader to give prompt obedience to the indications given him. The concentration of attention necessary can only come with practice. No end of surprises and amusement will follow if the operator honestly concentrates his mind upon the things to be done, and a good muscle-reader is found to take up the indications. Apparently, the most difficult feats are sometimes accomplished.

During the experiments, the reader will have curious sensations, such as heaviness of feeling, dread and uncertainty, and then *blankness* of mind, followed by an impulse to do something. If the reader can keep his mind passive enough, he may receive impressions, as in thought-transference; anyway, it is advisable to wait for the impulse to move and to do. The highest percentages of success always follow.

General directions for the cultivation of experimental thought-transference and mind-reading given in these pages are sufficiently specific, to be found thoroughly practical by those who have put them into practice; and certainly no harm, either mental or physical, can come to those who are willing to give them a fair trial.

CHAPTER VII.

Spiritualism.

Any reference to Spiritualism here must be very brief, and, I am afraid, very incomplete. I will deal with the subject in the light of the preceding chapters.

It has been established on the clearest evidence that thought-transference and reception between two nearly harmonised or sympathetic human beings, or embodied human spirits, are possible, and this without intermediate sense or physical agencies. If, then, between mind and mind on earth, distance or space being no obstacle, matter no hindrance, why not between mind disincarnate—if we can conceive of mind apart from the human brain and organism—and mind incarnate? If not, why not?

It seems to me very difficult, if we accept the first, to reject the latter conclusion. If we accept the latter, we are committed in the main to belief in Spiritualism, ancient and modern. If we admit that it is possible for a disembodied spirit to communicate with us in dream, vision, or, as in the case of Miss Howett, have our hands influenced to write, or that we see and converse with spirits, as in the case of Mary Reynolds, we then admit, and accept in the main, the essential features of what is known as Spiritualism. The subject is not only interesting, but of vital importance; therefore, I think, the fear of being called a "Spiritualist," or any other name, should not prevent us sounding to the depths, the psychic possibilities of our human nature.

THE SPIRIT WITHIN US.

There is Spiritualism *and* Spiritualism. That which I am most interested in is not so much a hankering after spirits, "spirit controls," and the phenomena, generally recognised as the right thing in certain circles, as that other Spiritualism which leads to an honest endeavour on our parts to ascertain if we are spirits, here and now, albeit clothed for the time being in an organic envelope, relating us to our present estate.

If we are embodied spirits, it will be possible for the spirit-man (the essential self—*ego*, I am), in each human being to communicate at times, and under certain fitting conditions, with other fellow-beings, under such circumstances, and in such a way, as to make it clear:—

(*a.*) That the communications could not have been transmitted and received by the ordinary channels, or physical sense organs, which in ordinary circumstances appear essential to our exchange of thought.

(*b.*) That the exchange of thought, in independence of the ordinary sense channels, will demonstrate that man must possess other, extraordinary or psychic, organs for the transmission and the reception of thought.

Both positions I have endeavoured to sustain on the foregoing pages; and, lastly, concerning spiritualism, I have arrived at the profound conclusion that spirit-communion—that is, thought transmission from the disembodied to the embodied—is a solemn fact. After carefully eliminating all the possibilities of self-deception—auto-trance, discreet degrees of consciousness, of natural and acquired clairvoyance, of thought-transference and mind-reading, and lastly, the puerile performances of conjurors and the simulated phenomena of tricksters—there remains evidence of disembodied or disincarnate spirit, and of such control influencing and directing the actions of men, just as one man in this life influences and directs the actions of another.

What I esteem, however, as satisfactory evidence might not be evidence to another; and I for one do not think it necessary to open up the life chambers of my psychic experiences to the indifferent, the thoughtless, or the sceptic, to furnish the desired evidence. Others must travel by the way I have come to understand something of that way. All men cannot believe alike, hence it will not be surprising that some will accept as sufficient evidence of spirit what others would deem insufficient.

It is not my intention meantime to advocate spiritualism. I only refer to it, in so far as it is related to "How to Thought-Read." However, phenomenal spiritualism is not a matter of belief so much as of evidence, and many eminent thinkers have been compelled by the force of the evidence to accept spiritualism now, who, a quarter of a century ago, would have hesitated, principally through fear of ridicule, to speak of the subject in language of ordinary civility.

While I am convinced that such communications between the so-called dead and the living are possible, I do know and feel satisfied that much which is accepted as evidence of the existence and influence of spirits by the majority of the unthinking and excitable crowd who rush after novelties, and perchance call themselves "spiritualists," is traceable to no other or higher source than our own innate, but little understood, human or psychic powers. I have arrived at this conclusion also, as the result of carefully investigating spiritualism, and it is therefore not an *a priori* hypothesis conveniently elaborated from my own or borrowed from the brains of others who are opponents to spiritualism. It is probable, had I not devoted the greater part of my life to spiritualism, as one of the factors in human character, I should have known but little of that sympathetic transference of thought from one mind to another, or of the light which that fact throws upon our dual or compound existence.

In this "sympathetic transference of thought" we find a solution to the problem of spiritualism, whether old or new. I conclude, with Buffon, "The true springs of our organisation are *not* these muscles, these veins, these arteries, which are described with so much exactness and care. There exist in organised bodies *internal forces* which do not follow the gross mechanical laws we imagine, and to which we would reduce everything." Or, as Laplace puts it more strongly—"Beyond the limits of this visible anatomy commences another anatomy, whose phenomena we cannot perceive; beyond the limits of this external physiology of forces, of action, and of motion, exists another *invisible physiology, whose principles, effects, and laws are of the greatest importance to know.*"

It may be esteemed reprehensible to "seek communion with the dead;" but to know ourselves, to fathom this *invisible physiology*, whose principles, effects, and laws are of such importance to understand, I hold to be not only legitimate but perfectly laudable. How can we serve God, whom we have not seen, if we do not understand ourselves, whom we think we have seen, or the laws which govern our being, as created by him? To know ourselves as we should, we ought not to neglect the search for "the spirit within us."

THE REJECTION OF THE PSYCHIC.

Many persons—scientific, theological, learned, and illiterate—reject the psychic, and refrain from investigating, either from constitutional bias or from crass ignorance; and such have played the part of learned Sadducees or low fellows of the baser sort before anything having the remotest flavour of spirit. The man of science is rendered purblind by "my hypothesis," the theologian by "my belief," the man of the world by "my business" or "my position." The respectable church-goer—who vaccinates his children, as he has them baptised, because it is the proper thing to do—has neither head nor heart, apparently, to understand anything beyond the common ideas of the hour. He would crucify all new thought, or new spiritualism for that matter, as the Jews did Jesus, because the new doctrines promulgated and the new wonders performed tend to subvert the present respectable order of things.

The worship of Diana is not confined to ancient Ephesus. The great Diana of old was the type of that "Respectable Custom" which the majority of mankind worship and obey to-day, because, as of yore, it conserves their vested interests, official connections, and brings them "much gain." As for the man in the street—the multitude having no shepherd—he is always more or less hypnotised by the well-clad and well-fed, smug-faced worshippers of the aforesaid "Respectable Custom;" hence he is ever ready to shout "Crucify," or "Hurrah," or aught else he is influenced to do, especially if such exercises give him pleasure and excitement for the time being. He accepts or rejects as he sees "his betters" think best, and so, unfortunately, is unfitted to a large degree, for the intelligent investigation of his own nature. These form the largest group of rejectors of the phenomenal evidences of soul.

The psychic, however, has suffered less from such rejectors than from those who claim to be recognised and known as converts and exponents of the same, who at best have only shown themselves to be "seekers after a sign." They may have run into the wilderness and have had a bit of miraculous bread, and yet not be a pennyworth the better of it in either soul or body—*i.e.*, life or conduct. These, by their foolishness, have prevented many well-meaning and otherwise able persons investigating the psychic, for the latter saw nothing in the lives of professed spiritualists to make them desire to have anything to do with spiritualism. Moreover, coming in contact with the iconoclastic in spiritualism, they have become disgusted with the crude and the coarse therein, as they have with the revelations, inspirations, and fads, advocated by certain mediums, and hence have rejected the wheat because of the apparent great quantity of tares.

THE FRAUDULENT IN SPIRITUALISM.

I am afraid the trend of modern civilisation, which leads men from the beauties and quietude of hill and dale, of valley and river side, into crowded city life, has tended to make men exoteric. They run after signs and wonders without, and too little to the spirit within. The broader view of being, and that self-culture and purity which arises from the exercise of man's innate powers, and makes for true regeneration and spiritual progress, here and hereafter, have been more or less sacrificed to the external and the phenomenal.

The love of the phenomenal, in and out of Spiritualism, has created a crowd of harpies, impostors, or fraudulent mediums—male and female—who trade on human credulity, some to earn a pittance, and others to gratify vanity. Men and women have been known to risk reputation for both. In this way Spiritualism has its quota of deceivers and deceived.

There are some people who must have phenomena, just as there are other people who will have sermons. If they don't get exactly what they want, they withdraw "their patronage"—the finances. So, if the patronage is to be retained, phenomena and sermons have to be supplied—if the first are fraudulent or the latter stolen.

Seeing how fugitive real psychological phenomena are—natural or induced—one must necessarily hesitate to accept "trance addresses," "inspirational orations," "medical controls," clairvoyant, and second-sight exhibitions, which are supplied to order, to gratify patrons, at so much per hour. It is human to err, but the manufacturer of spurious phenomena, the impostor who trades on the ties, and the dearest of human affections, is a devil. There is no iniquity too low—earthly or devilish—to which he will not as readily descend to gratify his vampirish nature.

I am not disposed to accept the infallibility of spirits for that of Popes—large or small—or professional media, in place of professional priests and ministers, and there is by far too much of this in Spiritualism.

In the foregoing connection, I must refer to another source of error—this time, however, more related to physical rather than psychic phenomena—viz., the credulity of those who are disposed to believe that certain conjurors are aided in their performances by spirit agency. Personally, I would sooner believe that mediums for "Physical Phenomena" resorted to conjuring to aid "spirits," than believe that "spirits" resorted to "hanky-panky" to aid conjurors. No wonder "frauds" smile. Years ago I had to protest against this absurdity, when people—who ought to know better—talked this kind of nonsense about conjurors, as they do about certain fraudulent mediums now—viz., "they are aided by spirits." Owing to this lack of discrimination and want of trained discernment in Spiritualists and the general public, mediumistic frauds have fooled, to their utmost bent, fresh groups of dupes at home and abroad.

I am none the less disposed to accept the genuine, because we recognise sources of error connected therewith, and are determined to set our faces against palpable frauds.

SPIRITUALISM WITHOUT SPIRITS.

We may now turn from the wretched arena of imposture, duplicity, and credulity, to genuine, but little understood, phenomena in Spiritualism. We have seen that much which has been attributed to the agency of disembodied spirits is due, in many instances, to the action of man's own psychic states, "the double, who is wiser than we," and to the fact that, as often as not, trance states, automatic and planchette writing, are self-induced conditions. Equally so, clairvoyance, thought-transference, and psychometry do not require the "agency of spirit" to account for their existence as "gifts," qualities or powers. It will be time enough to admit such agency—that of disembodied spirit—when the evidence in each particular case is reasonably conclusive. I think this is the only wise and safe course to pursue.

Clairvoyance may be native or induced, self-cultivated or cultivated by aid of a mesmerist. As it has been exercised naturally, and without any such aid, the exhibition of clairvoyance—in itself—is no evidence of disembodied spirit-presence or control. Equally, the seeing of, and the describing of, spirits by a clairvoyant—even if the descriptions are apparently accurate—may present no evidence of the real presence of such spirits. I do not deny that clairvoyants can see spirits, but the mere fact of being able to see and describe spirits, is not sufficient evidence—the *seer* is controlled by spirit-power to see, or that the spirits described are actually *bona-fide* spirits. Frequently, so-called spirits have no other existence than the image of them possessed by some positive-minded individual. A clairvoyant, *perceiving* these images, might naturally enough conclude she was actually seeing the spirits which she described.

If Mr. Stead, for instance, is convinced that "Sister Dora," "Cardinal Manning," or "Lord Tennyson," are at his side, in his rooms, influencing and directing his mind, or at other times actually controlling his arm and hand to write, a clairvoyant in sympathy with him may describe this or that other spirit he is *thinking* about. But that does not prove the spirit or spirits are actually present.

A lady (Mrs. Davis), whose name has come prominently before the public as Mr. Stead's clairvoyante, being questioned as to Mr. Stead's automatic writing and her own gift, said:—"I know probably more about that than anyone. I was in his office some time in the beginning of December last regarding the forthcoming publication of a book of mine concerning spiritualism. The conversation turned upon spiritualistic automatic handwriting. I did not know the deceased lady who was writing through him, but I saw her behind his chair as distinctly as if she had been in the flesh. I described her position as she stood and her appearance. She at once wrote through Mr. Stead's hand confirming all I had stated concerning her in my description. Mr. Stead's hand continued to write. I knew afterwards it wrote out a message stating that another spirit was in the room. Mr. Stead asked me if I could describe that spirit. I had to wait some little time before I detected it, and there I recognised as in the flesh a very famous personage recently dead, whose loss was mourned all the world over in prose and verse. I carefully described the spirit as he appeared to me, and then Mr. Stead said I was right. But, I answered, I see another male spirit. Ask the deceased lady who is writing through you to write the name of the last spirit. Mr. Stead's hand automatically moved, and he wrote the name of a son of the famous personage already alluded to." Mrs. Davis says she has been strongly impressed with the fact that Mr. Stead has been selected by the spirits as their champion from the peculiar and unique position he occupies in the journalistic world, and he will be the agent who will break through the solid walls of bigotry and prejudice. Mr. Stead may or may not have written under spirit influence, and this lady may or may not have seen spirits as described. We must not conclude in the latter case that Mr. Stead and his "trustworthy clairvoyante" are stating anything they do not believe to be true. I believe she saw, as described or thought of by Mr. Stead, a "deceased lady;" and that she also saw, as equally thought by him, "a very famous personage recently dead;" also "another male spirit," whose name she did not know until Mr. Stead wrote the name. This narrative, however interesting as to automatic writing and spirit agency in the opinions of those concerned, conveys no tangible evidence of either the one or the other. To us it is interesting in the fact that Mrs. Davis *saw the spirits thought of by Mr. Stead.* We must think twice before we can accept this as evidence of spirits and spirit-presence. Although it is possible those concerned have evidence, we have not. We have, however, evidence here of thought-transmission and psychic impressionability.

When we read of persons who have been raised up, as mediums of St. Peter, St. Paul, or St. John, or a publishing company being run by Shakespeare through a special medium, and worked by a syndicate of Spiritualists, I think we are entitled to doubt these claims, even though a dozen clairvoyants vouched for the existence and presence of the aforesaid spirits.

Psychometry furnishes evidence that many so-called spirits are not spirits "at all, at all"—only visions of the originals; and the fact that such and such an individual has been accurately described—actions and manners carefully indicated—and this has been and is accurately done in health and disease daily—is no evidence, in itself, that psychometers have seen spirits. Thus, when a psychometer places a geological specimen to his forehead, and describes an "antediluvian monster," roaring and walking about, no one but a very shallow individual would imagine for a second the psychometer was actually seeing the original. So many of the spirits and spectres seen do not proceed from our own brains, but from objects, relics, and old houses, which had been in times past impinged by the living presence and magnetism of the originals. Then we must take into consideration those spectres which proceed from our own brains, such as the realistic images which are sometimes projected from the background of consciousness to our eyes and ears. Many so-called spirits are simply the product of diseased neurological conditions, in short, hallucinations, which arise from some derangement of the optic and auditory centres. The spectres seen by Nicolai gradually disappeared as he lost blood, as the prescribed leeches tranquilised his system. We have no reason to believe the spectres he saw, visions and what not, were actually either spirits or produced by spirits.

MIND-READING IN SPIRITUALISM

is the commonest of most common experiences. I have known mediums to graphically describe scenes, persons, and incidents with such vividness as to impress one they must be controlled by spirits intimately acquainted with the whole circumstances which were revealed. Closer examination indicates that all the information so given by these mediums was based on the thought-read phase. That is, the information was culled from the minds of spirits in the flesh, and did not come from disembodied sources.

Some years ago I attended a series of seances in Liverpool. Nearly all the family were mediums of some sort. I was at this time very enthusiastic in my investigations. Consequently, the following incident was not lost upon me. One evening the circle met, with the usual members. Shortly after the circle was formed, the daughter of the house went into the trance state. There were several controls, one of whom professed to be a man who, the day before, had been injured on board one of Lambert & Holt's steamers, which lay in the Bramley Moore Dock. The "spirit" described the accident, how he was injured, and that he was carried to the hospital, and had "passed away." Owing to the suddenness of his death, he wished us to communicate with his family, and desired the circle to pray for him, etc. As near as I can recollect, when asked for further particulars, name, family, there was no definite reply. The medium quivered, and a new control had taken possession of her. I, however, neither doubted the *bona-fides* of the spirit nor the medium. I was especially interested in this control. I thought this time I had obtained a test of spirit identity. But alas for the imperfection of human hopes, I was doomed to disappointment. I clung to the idea the spirit would come back again, and when he got "more power," we would get the particulars he wanted to give us. He did not come back—and no wonder. Four months subsequently, I met the real Simon Pure in the flesh.

To explain more fully: On the day previous to the seance mentioned, I was on board the newly-arrived steamer in question. The lumpers were getting out the cargo. This man had been working on the top of the cargo in the main hold "hooking on." I paid no particular attention at the time to him, but an hour after I heard a great outcry, and saw a rush of men to the main hold. When I turned back and got there, I found this man senseless and bleeding.

The hooks had slipped off a bale while easing out some cargo. One of them had caught the poor fellow in the mouth, and had torn up his cheek almost to the right ear. He was to all appearance dying. I temporarily dressed his face, and the stevedore had him put on a stretcher and sent to the hospital. *I did not know his name or the hospital to which he was removed.* That day and the next the whole scene was vividly impressed on my mind. Hence that night the circumstances at the seance seem to me to be quite natural. Everything advanced was wonderfully apposite and convincing. It was not till I saw the man, and conversed with him, that my so-called test of spirit identity resolved itself into so much thought or mind reading, so that, even presuming the medium or sensitive was controlled by "a spirit," there can be no doubt the source of the spirit's information was purely mundane.

AUTOMATIC AND PLANCHETTE WRITING,

upon which so much reliance is placed, as furnishing evidence of "disembodied spirit control," presents similar difficulties. The recording of forgotten incidents, and predicting possibilities in the future, are not beyond the powers of the innate human spirit—wholly and utterly unaided by spirit agency. Therefore automatic writing—when genuine—does not necessarily furnish evidence of spirit control, not even when the person who writes believes, and honestly believes too, he is so controlled to write.

CHAPTER VIII.

SPIRITUALISM.—*Continued.*

AUTOMATIC writing is a phase of phenomenal Spiritualism most difficult to prove. In the majority of cases we are reduced to the awkward position of accepting or rejecting the assertions of the persons who declare that the writing done by them is automatic—that is, written without thought and volition on their part. A close examination of this claim may lead to the conclusion that automatic writing is not impossible. Whether the controlling agent is "the spirit within us," or a disembodied spirit, or both, is not a matter of much importance, if it is established, the writing is automatic. When messages are written without volition, in the handwriting of deceased persons, signed by their names, such messages must be treated on their merits. I have seen messages written in this way. I have seen messages written, not only automatically, but *direct*. Some were written the reverse way, and could only be read by holding up to the light or to a mirror. The direct writing was done in an exceedingly short time, two or three hundred words in less time than an expert phonographer could write the same by the most expeditious efforts. The evidence in favour of telepathic writing is not very strong, but of *direct* writing there appears to be abundant proof.

Dr. Nichols, in his fascinating work, "Forty Years of American Life," writes:—"I knew a Methodist sailor in New York, a simple, illiterate, earnest man, who became what is called a test medium. He came to see me in Cincinnati, and one evening we had also as visitors two distinguished lawyers: one of them a brother of Major Anderson, "the hero of Fort Sumter;" the other, a gentleman from Michigan, and one of the ablest lawyers practising in the Supreme Court of the United States. I had brought into the drawing-room a heavy walnut table, and placed it in the centre of the room. The medium sat down on one side of it, and the sharp Michigan lawyer, who was a stranger to us and the medium, on the other. The medium placed his fingers lightly upon the table. It tilted up under them, the two legs nearest him rising several inches. The lawyer examined the table, and tried to give it a similar movement, but without success. There was a force and a consequent movement he could not account for. There was no other person near the table, there was no perceptible muscular movement, and in no way in which it could be applied to produce the effect.

"When there was no doubt on this point, the lawyer, at the suggestion of the medium, wrote with careful secrecy on five bits of paper—rolling each up like a pea as he wrote—the names of five deceased persons whom he had known. Then he rolled them about until he felt sure that no one could tell one pellet from the other. Then, pointing to them successively, the tipping table selected one, which the gentleman, without opening, put in his waistcoat pocket, and threw the rest into the fire.

"The next step was to write the ages of these five persons at their death, on as many bits of paper, which were folded with the same care. One of these was selected, and again, without being opened, deposited in the lawyer's pocket, which now contained a name and a number indicating age.

"With the same precautions the lawyer then wrote, in the same way, on bits of paper, the places where these persons died, the diseases of which they died, and the dates of their decease, going through the same process with each. He had then in his pocket five little balls of paper, each selected by a movement of the table, for which no one could account.

"At this moment the hand of the medium seized a pencil, and with singular rapidity dashed off a few lines, addressed to the lawyer as from a near relative, and signed with a name which the medium very certainly had never heard.

"The lawyer, very much astonished, took from his pocket the five paper balls, unrolled them, spread them before him on the table, and read the same name as the one on the written message, with the person's age, the place and time of death, and the disease of which he died. They all corresponded with each other and the message. No person had approached the table, and neither lawyer nor medium had moved. It was in my own house, under a full gas light, and, so far as I could see, or can see now, no deception was possible.

"The written communication, which purported to come from a deceased relative of the gentleman only expressed, in affectionate terms, happiness at being able to give him this evidence of immortality."

This incident is introduced here in illustration of one out of many phases of mediumship known to spiritualists. We see here both psychic and physical powers-exercised, not generally recognised as possible. A massive table moved without physical leverage or exertion, and "thoughts read," which formed the basis of the message. Trickery and collusion in this instance are absolutely out of the question. The only questions which remain to answer are: "Did this medium possess in himself the powers referred to? or did he possess them in consequence of being controlled by a disembodied spirit, as claimed by the message?" Although the message in itself did not contain evidence of any other source of information than that emanating from the lawyer's own mind, we are forced to the conclusion that either the medium or the spirit controlling the medium had power to read his mind, and of exerting what Professor Crookes and Sergeant Cox would call Psychic Force to move the table, and indicate what pellets to select. We have here evidence of an intelligence capable of exercising an unknown force and of reading thoughts—that intelligence claimed to be a human spirit.

TRANCE ADDRESSES.

Trance and inspirational addresses, however, do not, in my opinion, furnish much evidence of the reality of spirit control. We are interested in the phenomena—taking for granted that these trance and inspirational states are genuine—although the evidence of external spirit control presented is often *nil*. The controls may or may not be veritable realities to their own mediums—professional or otherwise—but this is of little value, as evidence, to the public. I have known mediumistic and otherwise sensitive persons to be controlled—*i.e.*, taken possession of by their reading. One gentleman swallowed large doses of Theodore Parker. In time he thought of Parker, talked of Parker, and finally believed he was "inspired" by Theodore Parker. This gentleman had been a Unitarian before being a Spiritualist, and doubtless his mind had been broadened and brightened by his course of Theodore Parker; but beyond his own belief and the evident state of excitability he exhibited when speaking under this supposed control, there was actually no evidence of "spirit control" worthy of notice.

Mrs. Cora L. V. Tappan-Richmond, an inspirational medium, from America, delivered a series of remarkable addresses in this country about twenty years ago. These were published by J. Burns, of Southampton Row, Holborn, W.C. A young gentleman from Brighton heard and read the lectures, and finally budded forth as "an inspirational speaker." For a long time the public got nothing but the Tappan lectures diluted. We had the same marvellous, even flow, similar processes of reasoning, fertility of illustration, and unbounded capacity for assertion. No one dare say this person was not inspired by the spirits. It might have been a way the spirits had of breaking in their instrument, but I had a shrewd suspicion the young orator was controlled by his reading. I don't know how many others have been influenced in this way. I have noticed when a noted medium "came to town," delivered a number of addresses in public, or gave seances in private, immediately thereafter a number of imitators professed—correctly or otherwise—principally otherwise—to have been controlled by the guides, who were supposed to control the medium aforesaid, and that they would soon be able to give addresses and manifestations, and what not. On the other hand, the noted mediums averred "their guides never controlled any other than themselves," etc. The conscientious investigator is left to wonder how much imitation, vanity, and self-deception have to do with such statements.

Some of the most perfect oratory, and some of the ablest and most cogent lectures and addresses I have ever listened to have been given by trance and inspirational mediums. It was stated, as evidence of spirit control, by those who professed to know, "that these mediums could not reason and speak that way in their normal condition." All of which is worthy of consideration. At the same time I saw nothing inherently impossible—judging from a physiological or cerebral-physiognomic standpoint—to prevent these persons delivering, unaided by spirit agency, the addresses referred to. That a person speaks with greater ability, intelligence, or fluency in the trance state compared with his known powers in the waking state, cannot, alone, be accepted as proof of spirit control. We have seen hypnotised subjects do the same. But the reality, or otherwise, of spirit agency, cannot be estimated by the superiority, or otherwise, of the addresses and messages given.

In all public meetings and in seances where a medium is expected to give trance and inspirational addresses the platform is "supported" or the chair surrounded by sympathisers, whose presence is esteemed favourable to "good conditions"—a "nebulous term" better understood by Spiritualists than the public. When the address is, as is often the case, a miserable jumble of things inconsequential, old, experienced Spiritualists say it is owing "to bad conditions," *i.e.*, the influence of the audience on the speaker being conflicting and bad, hence the inconclusive rambling of the spirit's oration. Whether this is the true explanation or not, whether the medium was really controlled or not, or the addresses successful or not, the fact remains that Spiritualists admit that the "message" is not only "seriously modified," according to the channel (or medium) through whom it is given, but that it may be deflected and distorted by the influences of the audience to whom it is given. Whatever the real cause of the imperfect oratory, what is this but admitting *the thoughts transferred from the audience to the sensitive either make or mar the utterance*? If spirit utterance is thus influenced, it becomes a difficult matter to decide how much of the original message has reached us as intended, and how unwise it is for some to have their lives directed by such uncertain counsel.

There are many persons so organised, that when they come in contact with Spiritualism, (not knowing anything about clairvoyance, psychometry, thought-transference, thought-reading, etc.) are so convinced by what they hear and see for the first time—so much out of the ordinary run of their experience—the only way they can account for the phenomena is, "that they must be the work of spirits, for no human being could tell what they knew, or what they wanted, save a spirit who could read their thoughts." This is just where, I think, the error creeps in. Those very revelations which they in ignorance so readily attribute as only possible coming from disembodied spirits, may be and are in some instances quite possible to man, unaided by any such agency.

Many years ago I sat with Mr. David Duguid, the Glasgow painting medium. I had a "direct spirit painting" done. It was a correct—as far as I can recollect—painting of a small farm-house and stead, in the North of Ireland, where I as a child had been sent for my health. Neither Mr. Duguid nor the control claimed to possess any actual knowledge of me, or of the circumstances of my childhood. When I had an opportunity of attending the seance in question, I wondered if such a scene could be painted, and my wonder was greater when it was done.

Here again, we have evidence of thought-transference. Whether Mr. Duguid, by some occult power, caused the direct painting to be done—his own spirit doing it while his body was in the trance state—or the painting was produced by one of his controls, I am not prepared to state. I am willing to state my belief that the painting was not done by Duguid, the medium, or any other person present in the room. One of the controls of the medium claimed to have painted the little sketch, and, truth to tell, it is not more difficult to accept this hypothesis than "the spirit of the medium did it." In our ordinary experience of human nature, we do not find it usual for men to give credit to others—men or spirits—for what they are capable of doing and saying themselves.

REFLECTIONS.

It is quite possible, seeing that out of this life into the next, through the portals of death, pass all sorts and conditions of human beings, that in the next stage of existence—most closely allied to that in which we now live—mankind are not essentially different in character from what we find now. It is not, therefore, necessary to call in the agency of demons, as distinct from human spirits, to account for the phenomena of Spiritualism. If in artificial somnambulism and the phenomena of the psychic state the operating agent is an embodied human spirit, it is possible the same human spirit, albeit disembodied, may still retain power to control or influence other human beings.

There is another and more serious matter for consideration, concerning which our investigations of Spiritualism have thrown little or no light—Spirit Identity. Not only do our friends depart and never return, and many have promised to do so. How far are we certain when spirits have returned? We may have been deceived by our own impulsiveness, anxiety, and desire to feel and to know that "they are not lost but gone before." Again, admitting the genuineness of physical phenomena, and conceding that all the communications are really made by disembodied spirits or intelligent beings like unto ourselves, what proof do we possess that they are really what they represent themselves to be, or what they appear to be in spirit circles? "A bad or mischievous spirit," says Dr. Nichols, "may, for aught we know, personate our friends, *penetrate our secrets*, and deceive us with false representations." This is certainly worth thinking about. My object in writing is not to turn my readers against Spiritualism, but to get them to bring into the investigation judgment, not only to analyse evidence, but the capacity to "judge not according to appearance, but judge righteous judgment." It is no part of my purpose to deal with the history, ethics, or even the phenomena of Spiritualism. That has been well done by others. I merely write to show that Spiritualism "has something in it," and is of such importance that it is neither to be lightly rejected on the one hand, nor are its phenomena at all times to be attributed to agency of disembodied spirits.

Spiritualism is a many-sided subject, and too vast in its proportions to be dealt with here, and while I have no doubt that its public mediumistic exponents are no more perfect than the rest of humanity—much is laid at their door which may have a basis on fact—yet I do think they often suffer unjustly. Firstly, from the cries of the ignorant—educated or otherwise, matters little—who charge them with fraud, simply because such people are ignorant of the psychic possibilities of man; and, secondly, from the admiring and thoughtless many who are prepared to accept the commonest of psychic phases instanter as evidence of "disembodied spirit" presence and power. I have no doubt many phenomena are quite explicable on natural grounds. Setting aside the possibilities of self-deception in untrained observers, and of fraud in dishonest mediums, and of genuine phenomena traceable to the powers of the "spirit which is within each of us," there remains, to my mind, abundant evidence of the existence of "discarnate spirit," possessing all the attributes of the human spirit, as we know ourselves from the study of man as a psychological subject. Unfortunately, the very best evidence in favour of both "embodied" and "disembodied spirit" is not of that kind which is available for publicity. Still, I hold, if there is evidence (psychological and physical) for disembodied spirit in Spiritualism, I am also satisfied there is abundant evidence for embodied spirit in the psychological experiences of life, apart from what we know of Spiritualism.

I may fitly close these reflections by quoting the testimony of that keen scientific observer anent phenomenal Spiritualism—namely, Cromwell F. Varley, Esq., F.R.S:—"Twenty-five years ago I was a hard-headed unbeliever.... Spiritual phenomena, however, suddenly and quite unexpectedly was soon after developed in my own family.... This led me to inquire, and to try numerous experiments in such a way as to preclude, as much as circumstances would permit, the possibility of trickery and self-deception."... He then details various phases of the phenomena which had come within the range of his personal experience, and continues:—"Other and curious phenomena had occurred, proving the existence (*a*) of forces unknown to science; (*b*) *the power of instantly reading my thoughts*; (*c*) the presence of some intelligence or intelligences controlling those powers.... That the phenomena occur there is overwhelming evidence, and it is too late to deny their existence."

The Bibliography of Spiritualism is somewhat extensive. What books are best to recommend to beginners is not an easy matter to decide. "The Use of Spiritualism," by the late S. C. Hall, F.S.A.,[G] however, will repay perusal, and from the intellectual fitness, high moral tone, and spotless reputation of the author, this book may be safely recommended to all readers.

THEOSOPHY.[H]

I have been frequently asked, What is Theosophy? A question more easily asked than answered, and in answering I may do even less justice to it than to Spiritualism. Theosophy is an intellectual speculation, having for its main object the supplanting of Christianity, by a Revised Version of Hindoo Metempsychosis. An attempt to foist upon our western ideas and exoteric habits of thought, the mysticisms and esoteric speculations of the mystics of India and Japan. Modern Spiritualism is not a religion. Theosophy not only claims to be a religion, but to be "the essential basis of all religions." Modern Spiritualism may have its faults, and be as imperfect as human souls are here or hereafter. But we at least understand its faults and defects. The triple-crowned spiritual monarch—sitting on the seven hills of Rome—is not more infallible than the principles which underlie Theosophy—with its demi-gods, its Mahatmas, its adepts, miracle workers and wonders. To not understand and be able to accept these principles at once, is to proclaim oneself an ignoramus. Theosophy is a strangely fascinating religion for intellectual æsthetics.

Spiritualism is at least susceptible of being observed and investigated, and the hypothesis of Spiritualism is naturally a reasonable deduction from the facts. Not so Theosophy, which is merely a theory, an *a priori* assumption pleasing to those with more reflective and imaginative powers than capacity for practical observation. Spiritualism has given facts to be examined and tested, Theosophy nothing save gigantic and baseless assertions. Its *astral shells* and *elementals* are like its *Mahatmas*, flimsy phantasies, less tangible than the ghost seen and described by Dr. Jessop, or visions of the *shade of shades*, seen by psychometers. For these latter we have at least a basis in psychic phenomena.

Re-incarnation is the back bone of Theosophy, and Karma its necessary adjunct. The *Kismet* of Mahomet and the doctrines of election of Calvinism are not more inexorable than the *Karma* of Theosophy. *Karma* is a combination of earthly experiences and expiations of the soul of man in time, during its everlasting process of incarnating and re-incarnating in search of Wisdom, the Eternal Reality, and the final extinction of all *individuality* in the Nirvana. *Devachan* is the intermediate state of oblivion, in which *personality* is blotted out, and into which the spiritual soul, etc., enters between the periods of incarnation.

Theosophy—the Wisdom of God religion—attempts to explain all the inequalities of life, the intellectual and moral differences in men, of sin and suffering, by its working theory, *Re-incarnation*, which doubtless has many attractive features.

The phenomena Theosophists place so much reliance upon are the property of mankind—somnambulism, psychic consciousness, clairvoyance, psychometry, thought-transference, etc. The "Theosophic miracles of communication with persons in other parts of the world" are explicable by thought-transference, and in time may be no more inherently impossible than telegraphy without wires and poles. The physical wonders of Theosophy, akin to those of Spiritualism, are attributed to *shells*, the *astral* carcases of once embodied but now rapidly dissolving *personality* of man, and *elementals*, fragmentary spirit imps or sprites, who up to the present have not been as yet incorporated in some incarnated human soul.

As to the ethics of Theosophy, brotherly kindness, charity, and self-sacrifice—most desirable virtues and *divine* attainments—are neither new nor the special property of Theosophy. Such *divine* qualities and virtues are common to all religions and religious teaching, and if they ever reached their climax in human form, they did in the person of Jesus, the Lord's Christ. He was the embodiment of these, and a living example for all time, long, long before unthinkable and "ungetatable" Mahatmas were announced by Madame Blavatsky, or believed in by Mrs. Besant.

Theosophists recognise seven distinct parts in man, *i.e.*, four transitory and three eternal. The transitory elements are—the physical body, the vital principle, the *astral body*, and the *animal soul*. These four comprise man's *personality*, and being transitory are perishable. Hence the *personality* of man is annihilated at death. The three eternal elements are—the *spirit*, the *spiritual soul*, and the *mind*. These being imperishable form man's *individuality*, and constitute the immortal part of man. This immortal part *incarnates* and *re-incarnates* throughout innumerable personalities on this globe, and the rest of the planets, beside having alternate periods of "rosy slumber" and of activity. Our *individuality* has no sex, consequently we may be a little negro wench in one incarnation, an Egyptian monarch in another, a Nero in another, a John Knox in another, and so on. Others may not progress, but sink from incarnation to incarnation, from a mother in Israel, to a Deeming in Australia, and, finally, to utter annihilation. Those good souls who *live the life*, and perfect their souls through much suffering, will become as one with "the Eternal Reality, the Rootless Root of all that was, or is, or ever shall be." The higher and ever advancing Theosophist may, however, stop short before he reaches the Nirvana, and elect to become a Mahatma, or great soul, and reside on this or some other planet to exercise power and precipitate wisdom, by letters and otherwise, to the world, through chosen adepts. The good Theosophist in this world and the next is surrounded by "thought-forms," which influence him in his upward career. The Spiritualist has his departed friends for guides, and the Christian (Spiritualist) is comforted by "messengers sent forth to minister to them that are heirs of salvation." I don't know that "thought-forms" administering counsel to a spirit having no *personality* is an improvement on the old ideas.

It is impossible to do justice to this Wisdom-Religion with its orders, grades, and bewildering phraseology. It is a fancy religion for the intellectual, without a personal God or a personal soul. Its circles are masonic lodges for the rich. In no sense is it a religion to meet the wants of man as man, like that founded on the life and death of Jesus Christ. I do not pretend to explain Theosophy, for the task is beyond me. It is a religion intended for those who realise they are divine sparks of the Rootless Root, and not for the common people, who are incapable of understanding a system of morals thus veiled in allegory, and illustrated by signs and symbols. Amid the perplexities of many words, we learn that Theosophy teaches what St. Paul indicates as the divine order of morals by the words: "Whatsoever a man soweth, that shall he also reap." To work out one's own salvation is as old as the race. We may all be Theosophists without knowing it, as we don't know who we are, what we were, or who we are going to be, such is *Karma*. Spiritualism and Theosophy are only referred to here seeing how largely the phenomena on which they are based, is explained by "How to Thought-Read."

CPSIA information can be obtained
at www.ICGtesting.com
Printed in the USA
BVHW021403180423
662562BV00015B/691

Ching-I Peng
1950.06.30~2018.05.01

EDUCATION

- B.S., Botany Department, National Chung-Hsing University, Taichung, Taiwan, 1972
- M.S., Botany Department, National Taiwan University, Taipei, Taiwan, 1976
- Ph.D., Biology Department, Washington University, St. Louis, Missouri, USA, 1982

APPOINTMENTS AND EXPERIENCE

- Executive Director, Thematic Center for Systematics and Biodiversity Informatics, Research Center for Biodiversity, Academia Sinica, Taipei, 2004-2018
- Research Fellow, Institute of Botany, Academia Sinica, Taipei, 1987-2004
- Associate Research Fellow and Herbarium Curator, Institute of Botany, Academia Sinica, Taipei, 1982–1987
- Research Assistant, Institute of Botany, Academia Sinica, Taipei, 1978
- Research Assistant, Yangmei Branch, Taiwan Livestock Research Institute, 1976–1977
- Academic Deputy Director, National Museum of Natural Science, Taichung, Taiwan, 1995–1997
- Acting Director, National Museum of Natural Science, Taichung, Taiwan, 1996–1997
- Adjunct Associate Professor, National Taiwan Marine College, 1983–1984
- Adjunct Associate Professor, National Taiwan Normal University, 1986–1987
- Adjunct Professor, National Taiwan Normal University, 1987–1989
- Director, Botanical Garden, National Museum of Natural Science, Taichung, Taiwan, 2003-2006
- Research Fellow, Research Center for Biodiversity, Academia Sinica, Taipei, 2005-2015
- Director, Biodiversity Research Museum, Academia Sinica, Taipei, 2007-2015
- Curator of Herbarium (HAST), Academia Sinica, Taipei, 1983-1995; 1998-1999; 2003-2015
- Adjunct Professor, National Cheng-Kung University, 2002-2016

AFFILIATIONS

- Taiwan Society of Plant Systematics, 2006-2018
- Botanical Society of the Republic of China, 1983–2018
- International Association for Plant Taxonomy, 1985–2018
- American Society of Plant Taxonomists, 1979–2018

EDITORIAL

- Co-Editor in Chief, Botanical Studies, 2007-2018Associate editor, Botanical Studies, 2006
- Associate editor, Botanical Bulletin of Academia Sinica, 1996 –2005
- Editor-in-Chief, Botanical Bulletin of Academia Sinica, 1992–1995
- Editorial board, Flora of China, 1997–2013
- Editorial board, Acta Phytotaxonomica Sinica (Beijing, China), 2004-2007
- Editorial board, Journal of Systematics and Evolution (Beijing, China), 2008-2018
- Editor, Acta Phytotaxonomica eobotanica (Japan), 1994–2018
- Editorial Board, Guihaia (Guangxi, China), 2001-2018
- Managing editor, vol. 4, Flora of Taiwan, 2nd edition, 1996–1998
- Advisory editorial board, Taiwan Journal of Forest Science, 1996 –2018
- Editorial consultant, Environmental Education Quarterly (Taiwan), 1996 –2018
- Associate Editor, Chromosome Science (Japan), 1999–2018
- Editor, Index to Plant Chromosome Numbers, 1984 – 2018

COMMITTEES/COUNCILS

- Council member, Taiwan Society of Plant Systematics, 2006-2018
- Council member, Botanical Society of the Republic of China, 1985–2018
- Council member, International Association for Plant Taxonomy, 1999-2005
- Council member (1991–) and Executive Secretary, ROC Committee of the Pacific Science ssociation, 1991–1995
- Council member (1992–) and Executive Secretary, ROC Committee of the International Union of Biological Sciences, 1992–1995
- Council member, Society of Wildlife and Nature ROC, 1997–2018
- Council member, Biological Society of China, 1999–2018
- Advisory board, Taiwan Endemic Species Research Institute, 1992–2018
- Advisory board, Taiwan Forestry Research Institute, 1996–2018
- Advisory board, National Museum of Natural Science, 1998–2018

SCIENTIFIC SYMPOSIA ORGANIZER

- Symposium on Plant Resources and Landscape Conservation, Taipei, 1987
- Workshop on the Biological Resources and Information Management of Taiwan, 1991
- ROC-USA Symposium on Phytogeography and Botanical Inventory of Taiwan, 1992
- International Symposium on Biodiversity and Terrestrial Ecosystems, Taipei, 1994
- International Symposium on Rare, Threatened, and Endangered Floras of Asia and the Pacific Rim, Taipei, 1996
- Workshop on Application of Information Systems on Botanical Inventory, Taipei, 1996
- Workshop on the Botanical Inventory of Taiwan (I), Taipei, 1996, Workshop on the Botanical Inventory of Taiwan (II), Taichung, 1997
- Cross-strait Symposium on Floristic Diversity and Conservation, Taichung, 1997
- Year 2000: Cross-strait Symposium on Biodiversity and Conservation, 2000
- International Symposium on the Future of Biodiversity in Taiwan, Taipei, 2000
- International Symposium on Plant Biodiversity and Development of Bioactive Natural Products, Taichung, 2001
- International Symposium: Frontiers in Plant Science, Taipei, 2002
- 2003 International Symposium on Plant Diversity in Eastern Asia and Workshop on Botanical Gardens, Taichung, 2003
- 2004 International Symposium on Plant Diversity, Taipei, 2004

TABLE OF CONTENTS

- 1   **Begonia and Me**
- 2   **Distribution**
- 6   **The habitat of the begonia**
  - Habitat: Rock walls
  - Habitat: limestone cave mouth
  - Habitat: next to the waterfall
- 12   **Characteristics of Begonias: standing upright and climbing trees**
- 15   **My first love**
- 17   **REPRODUCTIVE LIFE OF THE BEGONIA**
  - Pollinated Begonia
  - Asexual reproduction
  - Ease of hybridization and expression of dominant genes
- 25   **Begonia cultivation**
  - How Dr. Rekha Morris cultivates Begonia?
- 27   **Special uses for the begonia**
  - Uses in folk medicine
  - Use in beverages
  - Air purification
  - Other uses: Pig feed
  - Other interesting uses
- 35   **Begonia research**
  - Field studies are essential to and extremely important
  - New species found in a floral market?
- 39   **Food, clothing, lodging and transportation during field collection**
  - Eating in the wild
  - Lodgings: "Full star" accommodations
  - Transportation: a basketful of surprises
- 44   **Trekking in Search of Begonia**
  - The Philippines: A harmless surprise
  - Guizhou: Beauty, snakes, and fractures
  - Sabah, Malaysia: Bee stings
  - Pain experience
  - Guangxi: Climbing up a rock wall to find new varieties
  - The Philippines: new species found

Begonia and Me

Many people ask me why I like begonias. In the early Qing dynasty, historian Zhang Wei once said, "You can't make friends with those who have no hobby because they don't have deep feelings." Only a person with hobbies can know true love. Throughout my life, my heart will always be thinking of and searching for begonias. The begonia family has 1963 published species, growing throughout the world. But I believe there are many more out there to be found. The begonias we grow in the greenhouse are just one small selection of them. The diversity in begonias can be observed mainly in the leaves; in their shape, pattern variation, and thickness. All of these aspects can vary greatly. Begonias are so amazing and varied that it's no wonder they fascinate many, and cause some to obsess over finding every possible way to obtain them.

Distribution

Begonias are distributed in the tropics and subtropics to the north and south of the equator. It is not that begonia dislikes hot environments. Instead, they are afraid of the cold. In the north temperate zone, or wherever latitudes or altitudes are too high, begonias are unable to withstand the cold weather and will not survive.

There are nearly 2,000 published begonia species in the world, including 800 species in Central and South America, 200 in Africa and 800 in Asia. In North America, there are no natives in the United States or Canada. In Asia, there are more than 200 species in China and about 20 species in Taiwan, of which there are currently 19 on record. The 200 species in China are mainly distributed across the Yangtze River. Most often, my friends and I visited the river basin, in Yunnan and Guangxi, the hot spots of begoina.

Although the number of begonias found in Africa is less than that in Asia and the Americas, research shows that Africa is the origin of begonia. The route of begonia's ancient spread across the globe began from Africa to the Indian subcontinent thence to the Asian continent, Taiwan, and Southeast Asia.

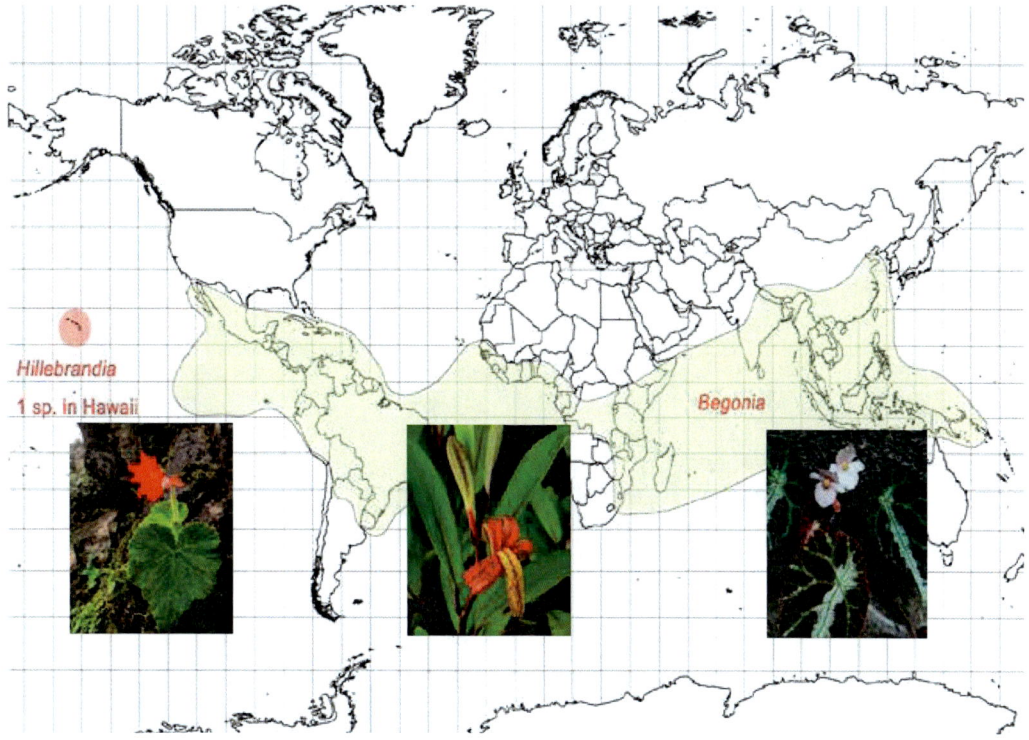

One kind of begonia, *Begonia grandis* ("秋海棠" in Chinese), whose leaf shape resembles the map of the Republic of China. It is one of the most widely distributed species in the world, thriving in mainland China from southern Guangdong to Shandong and Shanxi to the northeast and Liaoning. *Begonia grandis* is characterized by its strong adaptability, enabling it to survive anywhere from the subtropical to the northern temperate zone. Even near the cold zone, one can see traces of its existence.

In 2015, we announced that *Begonia grandis* found in Pingtung, southern Taiwan, adding a black dot to the Begonia map in Taiwan. It's a pity that, after a big typhoon, a landslide destroyed this location. Hopefully, the begonia will reappear, there, one day.

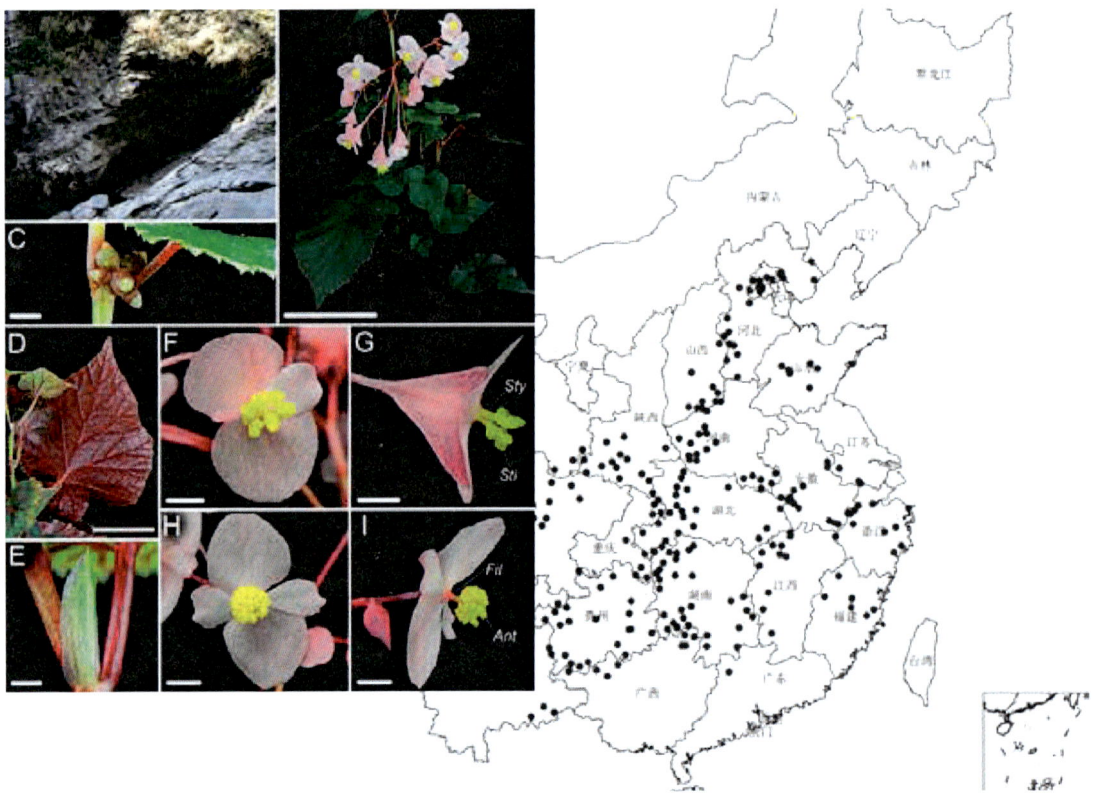

Distribution of *Begonia grandis* in China (Daike Tian, 2014)

The Map of the Republic of China Begonia, Lesson 34 in the textbook of the late Qing Dynasty, points out that China's topography resembles the begonia leaf, with the eastern part being its stems, west to the top of the ridge being its tip, and the provinces and protectorates forming the whole leaf.

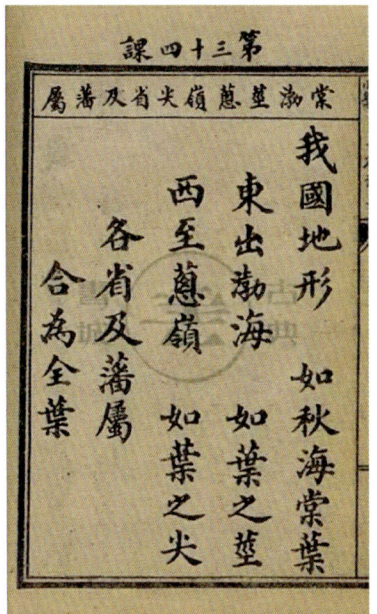

Why is the begonia called Qiu Haitang (秋海棠) in Chinese? A story written 800 years ago, in the Song dynasty explains it as follows:

(Yun Shouping, 1686)

> Once there was a woman who missed her husband. Often when they didn't see each other the woman would weep, shedding tears at the northern wall. Afterward, very charming flowers would appear, with petals the color of a woman's flushed cheeks. Its leaves green on top and red underneath, the flower blossoms in autumn and is named 'the broken hearted flower,' also known as 'Spring in August.'
>
> ~ Song dynasty, Miscellaneous Notes from Cai Lan

"The broken-hearted flower." Why is it also called "Spring in August"? Because, generally, we think spring's warmth open flowers.

""The northern wall" is appropriately mentioned, as that wall faces a northern slope, and begonias prefer cool and shady places. So, when I am trekking in the field, I often take a look at the compass, face the northern slopes, and stop there to look for begonias.

The habitat of the begonia: indicators of healthy forest ecosystems

Because begonias require high environmental stability, they are difficult to find in disturbed forests. Thus, the presence of begonias is often regarded as an indicator of a healthy forest ecosystems. Begonias like to grow in a cool, moist, slightly sheltered environment. They are commonly found along the forest floor, wet rock walls and waterfall edges.

Begonia blancii

Habitat: Rock walls

In the picture below, you'll notice a lizard next to the begonia on this rock wall. Do lizards also enjoy begonias? Not really, but the fragrance of begonia flower will attract insects, which delight lizards.

Begonia murina (Photograph by: Chien-I Huang)

For the scientist, "seeing is believing". In the Erawan National Park, Thailand, my assistants are very happy because there are not only many kinds of plants, but also beautiful scenery, attracting many foreign visitors. We pick begonias and take photos. In the picture below, my assistants took the picture while I focus on collecting begonias.

Habitat: limestone cave mouth

Most begonias are very narrowly distributed, so we say there is "one species to a mountain, one species to a hole, and one species to a valley". The "hole" here is actually a cave — a limestone cave.

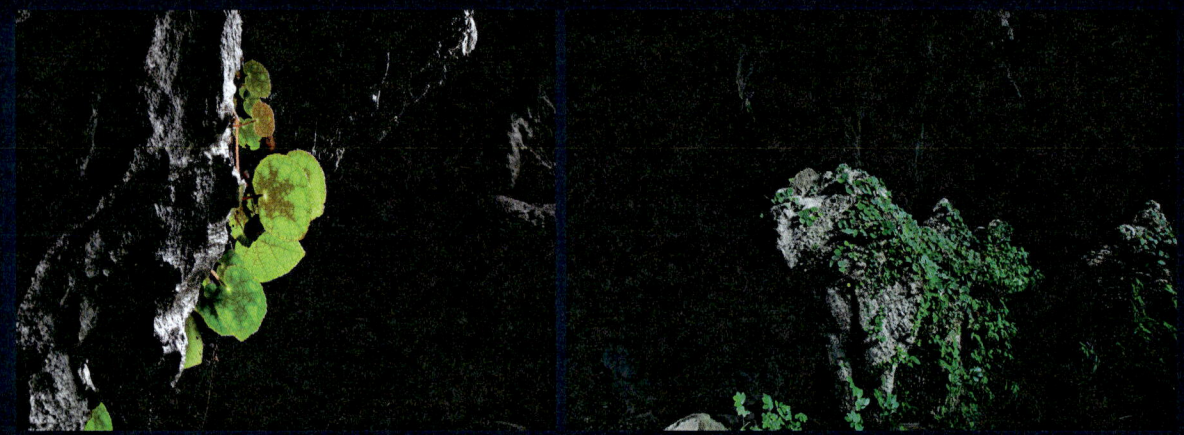

In Jingxi at the mouth of a karst limestone cave in Guangxi. It took me ore than an hour before I finally came away with a very beautiful picture of *Begonia picturata*.

Begonia picturata

The begonias seen here are basically growing inside the stone's cevices. Contrary to what most people may think, the inside of the crevices is quite moist. There are often invisible rivers under the stones.

After rain, the water will accumulate inside the stone's crevices, but not too much, so the begonias like this environment. When we cultivate them later, we should also consider their preferred environments.

Begonia luzhaiensis

Habitat: next to the waterfall

Some begonias, such as *Begonia leprosa* also like to grow next to waterfalls. Its leaf shape varies greatly.

Begonia leprosa

Characteristics of Begonias: standing upright and climbing trees

Is begonia tall or short?

The American Begonia Association invited me to give a speech at the annual convention to talk about the begonias of Taiwan and China. One photo drew much attention, prompting someone on the Internet to ask just how tall this beautiful begonia was. Someone replied, "This is Dr. Peng Ching-I from Taiwan. He is about five feet tall." This is certainly not true, five feet is only 150 centimeters! I became a dwarf. But then again, in front of the gorgeous Begonia, I really am relatively short. Is begonia tall or short?

"This is with Dr. Ching-I Peng from Taiwan (He is about five feet tall and was one of the keynote speakers at the convention about Taiwanese and Chinese begonias). So how tall do you think this begonia is?"

Begonia luxurians and me

Generally, the growth characteristics of begonias are divided into cane type and rhizomatous type, but in some parts of the world there are begonias that will climb trees. For example, in the tropical island of Luzon, Philippines, I saw the *Begonia megacarpa* in the rain forest growing on the forest floor, and just like the Devil's ivy, it can climb trees.

Begonia ceratocarpa

Begonia dipetala

Begonia megacarpa

Another begonia that will climb trees is *Begonia fagifolia*. At the Taipei Flower Expo in the Pavilion of Future, we exhibited it for many years. While we only planted it on the ground, it climbed its way up along the wooden window by itself.

Begonia fagifolia is from Brazil. It is a climbing plant with hairy branches favoring a semi-shadowed and humid environment. There are several ways to cultivate it—one is to plant it on the ground and let it climb as it likes, though this won't do in a greenhouse. Or you can provide a branch for it to climb. But you should sprinkle it with water often. Or, as shown below, you can use a bowl-sized coconut fiber pot and hang it.

Begonia fagifolia

My first love

My journey with Begonia began from the discovery of *Begonia ravenii*.

Begonia ravenii, growing in the south-central part of Taiwain. *Ravenii* passes the dry season in the form of tubers, hidden beneath the soil. Spring rains invite its re-emergence, and foster growth. Then summer and autumn days are brightened by *ravenii*'s beautiful flowers.

People always ask me how I got into researching begonias. Shortly after I had returned from the United States, I wanted to begin researching Taiwanese plants. One dry winter day, Dr. Yan Xinfu took me to Chiayi to see the begonias fruit hanging on the wall and they didn't have even a single leaf. I became very curious and checked existing literature, which at the time held no record of Taiwan's dormant and deciduous begonias. All the information indicated that begonias are evergreen, not deciduous, so I invested a lot of time in researching, checking previous literature, asking for support, and finally confirmed that this was an undocumented native Taiwanese species!

I dedicated the first new species of Begonia I discovered in Taiwan to Prof. Peter Raven, my mentor at Washington Univ. (St. Louis, USA)

Winter, dry season   Spring, rainy season   Summer & Autumn

As a small token of my gratitude and respect to Prof. Peter Raven, I presented a Chinese painting of *Begonia ravenii*, a handsome species endemic to Taiwan. This is the first new species of Begonia that I published (in 1988)

The writing says:

> The academic achievement of Prof. Raven, my mentor, is admired the world over. Prof. Raven has a deep affection for Chinese, and has visited Taiwan on many academic occasions, which we appreciate most profoundly. As a small token of my gratitude and respect to Prof. Raven, I present this Chinese painting of Begonia ravenii, a handsome species endemic to Taiwan, which I named in honor of him.
>
> Respectfully,
>
> Ching-I Peng
> Academia Sinica, Taipei
> Dated April 4, 2009

REPRODUCTIVE LIFE OF THE BEGONIA

How to identify begonias

- Frequently perennial, juicy herbs (tastes sour)
- Creeping rhizome or tuber
- Single leaf asymmetry, crooked base, alternate phyllotaxy (rarely palmately compound leaf)
- Single flower, monoecious (rarely dioecious), often male flowers open first
- The palate is petal-shaped (generally called "Tepal"); the male tepal is often 4 pieces, decussate. Female tepal 2-6 pieces of different size
- Abundance of stamens, clustered flowers
- Lower ovary, usually 2 or 3 chambers; abundance of ovules
- Dried, cracked winged capsular fruit, rarely berry fruit (ex. *Begonia hayatae*)
- The seeds are abundant and fine like dust

90% of the species are monoecious

Over 90% species of Begonia are monoecious, i.e., bearing male and female flowers on the same plant.

The male and female homologous Monoecious means that the female flowers and male flowers are all on the same plant. The obvious distinguishing feature of the female flower is the ovary, from which the fruit develops. Often the female flower will sag, while there is no swelling or bulging behind the male flower.

Begonia peltatifolia

Begonia wangii

Most of the stamens are crowded in the center of the flower's heart, and the female flower's ovary is underneath —a very important feature to know about the begonia; there are 2 or 3 chambers inside, with many ovules. Usually the female flowers will sag and the fruit will crack after ripening, giving way to a capsule with wings, berry-like in a few species, such as Taiwan's *Begonia longifolia*. The seeds are very fine, like dust, and come in large quantities.

Begonia longifolia

Pollinated Begonia

Begonia flowers do not produce nectar. Nonetheless, they require insects to effect pollination. Pollen is transferred by bees or other insects in nature. In the picture below, the top is a male flower. The insects flying over it are not collecting honey —the purpose of their visits is to collect pollen. Of course, it is useless to fly between male flowers, but sometimes they fly to female flowers, thus achieving pollination.

On the left is also a male flower, where the pollen is coming out from the left side. Male flowers have only a bunch of stamens. Female flowers usually have stigmas, styles, and an ovary. The ovary is now covered by a tepal. The stigma usually consists of two or three lobes.

The stigma of the begonia after pollination, observed under an electron microscope. The pollen bores thousands of holes into the top and germinates the stigma, binding to the ovule.

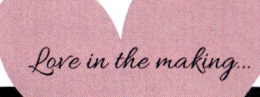

In nature, unisexual flowers must be pollinated with the help of insects, but in the greenhouse we often use artificial pollination. After six to eight weeks, the fruit will mature and split, and the seeds will fall out from the gaps. When the wind blows the seeds fall nearby, enabling the plant to multiply. Seeds can be planted about 6 to 8 weeks after pollination. The seeds of begonia are as small as dust, about 0.3mm to 0.6mm. Seeds from the lateral membrane group are relatively large and can be close to 0.6 mm and 0.7mm. When a single fruit is planted, the seedlings will grow in a dense pack.

Ease of hybridization and expression of dominant genes

Begonias are very easy to cross, especially in the same country or on the same continent. But it will be difficult to hybrid across continents. In the case of simple artificial hybridization, almost every group can be mated with another species. But in nature, with geographical barriers or differences in climate between caves, and hybridization is not so easy.

We have artificially crossed the *Begonia bamaensis* with *Begonia ningmingensis*, and the results were very interesting. The leaves are almost entirely white. The veins of the *Begonia bamaensis* are white and the *Begonia ningmingensis* is white along the veins. The fact that the hybrid's veins are almost all white is a clear expression of the dominant genes.

Begonia ningmingensis   *Begonia bamaensis*

At low altitude regions in the Himalayan mountains, there is a very important native species, *Begonia rex*, which is often used for horticultural breeding. It is called Hama Begonia ("toad" begonia) in Taiwan, or Dawang Begonia ("king" begonia) in mainland China. It is distributed across southwestern China, India, North Vietnam and Myanmar. It is an important native species, which is crossed with more than 500 wild begonias and produces thousands of ornamental garden varieties.

The hybridization of the Dawang Begonia has produced many excellent varieties. In the Royal Horticultural Society of the United Kingdom, there are special competitions for this every year. For example, one year's nominees included Pink Champagne, Silver King, Chinese Curl, Plate Snail, Sea Monster, Midnight Magic, Anyway, the name obtains. The more unusual or dazzling the name, perhaps the easier to impress the jury!

Red numbers in the text refer to these cultivars of Begonia Rex Cultorum Group:
1. Begonia 'Pink Champagne'
2. B. 'Silver King'
3. B. 'Roi de Roses'
4. B. 'China Curl'
5. B. 'Regal Minuet'
6. B. 'Rocheart'
7. B. 'Midnight Magic'
8. B. 'Escargot'
9. B. 'Sea Serpent'
10. B. 'Silver Cloud'
11. B. 'Dewdrop'
12. B. 'Fireworks'
13. B. 'Ironstone'
14. B. 'Carolina Moon'
15. B. 'Helen Lewis'

Asexual reproduction

In addition to sexual reproduction, some begonias have bead buds and tubers or bulbs, enabling asexual reproduction.

Begonia grandis

Looking at the *Begonia fimbristipula*, you can see asexual buds growing on the edge of its leaves.

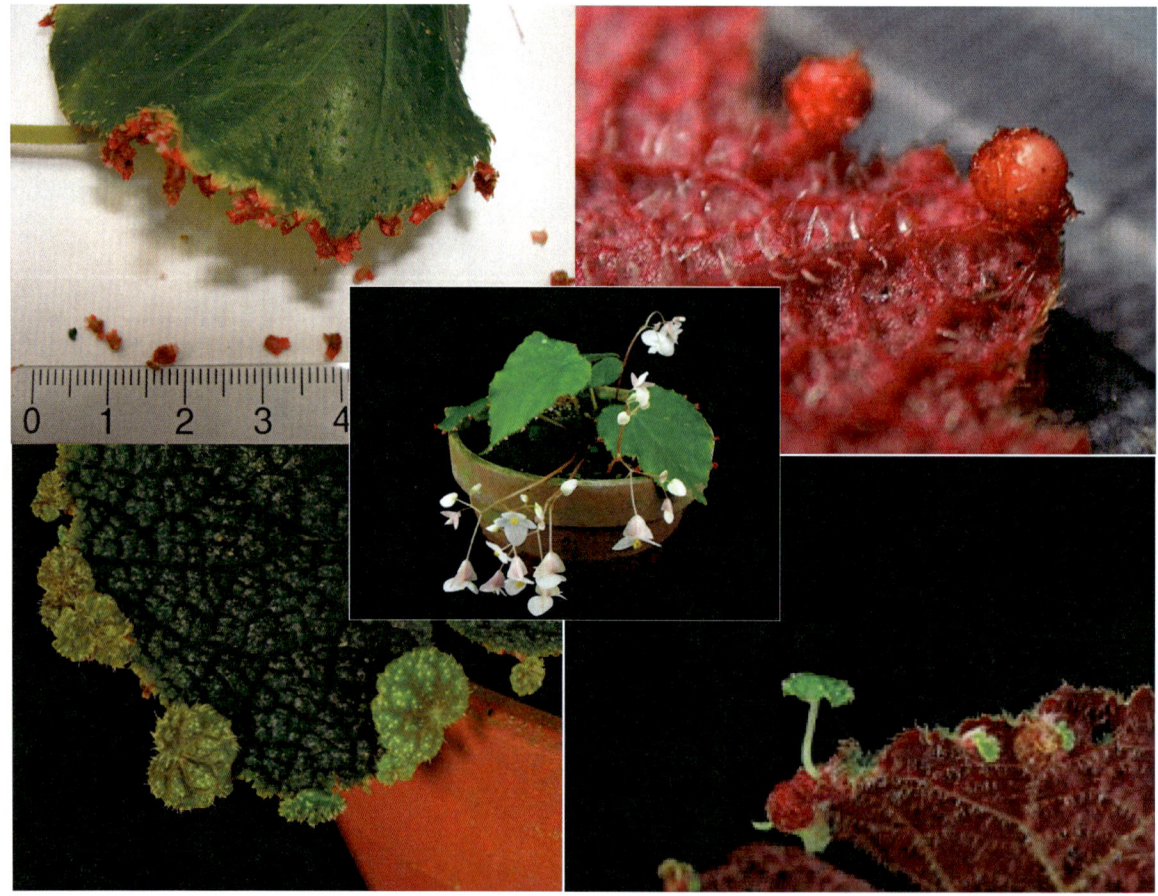

Begonia fimbristipula

Asexual reproduction of begonias can also be realized by a method called leaf-cutting. Cutting the leaves of *Begonia pulvinifera* in half and covering the moss with plastic bags will cause roots to grow.

Some species of begonia also grow roots under high humidity, even without leaf cutting.

Begonia pulvinifera

Begonia augustinei

Begonia cultivation

DOS
- Use a ventilating medium
- Keep cool in a shaded place in summer
- Move to a bright place in winter
- Provide a high humidity environment

DONT'S
- Don't place in direct sunlight
- Don't allow water to accumulate
- Don't fertilize heavily
- Don't keep in a drafty place

 On top of the above, add tender loving care.

The main points of begonia cultivation are the following: basically, begonias like a little ventilation without too much wind, so the use of a fan is unnecessary. Begonias also cannot be kept too wet nor too dry and should not be stored in an airtight environment. It is recommended to use a ventilated medium, keeping them in a cool place in the summer and a bright place in the winter when it is cold. In a high humidity environment, they must not be placed under direct sunlight, nor can water be permitted to accumulate. Also do not fertilize them heavily, or keep them in drafty places. On top of all the above, we must add tender loving care; to use a phrase in the local Hokkien dialect, ka-de-wu-bui, (literally, "the fat is on the soles of one's feet"), meaning diligence and extra care is the best fertilizer. There is a story behind this, actually. After graduating from my masters program, I worked at the Animal Production Laboratory for an ecological experiment as my first job. At the time, a specialist from the COA told us that we university students and research students must not consider ourselves superior to farmers because of our higher education. After all, the farmer that toils in the field every day can understand everything about his or her crops' conditions with every trip, and if there are any problems, they deal with them on the spot. "You students, on the other hand," he said, "probably just come once a month to scatter a little fertilizer, only to discover the next month that a lot of plants have died, or maybe been eaten by insects—and you don't even know what happened!" Instead, he added, "'ka-de-wu-bui'—the fat/fertilizer is on the soles of our feet!" So he admonished us to be as diligent and attentive as possible—like any farmer.

How Dr. Rekha Morris cultivates Begonia?

I visited my American friend Dr. Rekha Morris at her house once to see her collection of begonias. She has an indoor swimming pool, so the surroundings are very humid. She doesn't actually swim there, but she does plant all of her begonias next to the pool, where they can enjoy the most suitable growing environment.

Dr. Rekha Morris, a dear friend of mine and a specialist on Eurasian Art History, has a keen interest on Begonia. Notwithstanding the difficult terrains and potential dangers, she made many field expeditions for begonias in Central and South Americas as well as the Himalayas. She and I have frequent academic exchanges and she generously offers me many rare and precious Begonias for study from time to time. I am truly indebted to her for the enduring friendship and I admire her profound knowledge on begonias. As a small token of my profound appreciation, I took the opportunity of a trip to USA to present her this Chinese water color painting of *Begonia pengii*, which I hope she enjoyed.

Begonia pengii
(photograph by Yan Liu)

Special uses for begonia

Uses in folk medicine

What purpose do begonias serve in addition to bringing aesthetic pleasure? In some folk medicine traditions certain types of begonia, such as the *Begonia grandis*, are said to help hemostasis and hold detoxification and antidiarrheal functions; the *Begonia longifolia* can be used for treating burns and snake bites; and the *Begonia cathayana* can relieve coughing, inflammation and bronchitis.

Begonia grandis

Begonia longifolia

Begonia cathayana

Use in beverages

In Lanyu (Orchid Island), *Begonia fenicis* is used to make salad. It has a sour taste, so some mayonnaise dressing can make it taste delicious. It can also be made into a smoothie with a special texture.

begonia salad

Begonia fenicis

In mainland China, Begonia leaves are used to make a tea that tastes like roselle tea. Ten years ago, when I first visited Guangdong, the price was about 230 yuan for every half kilogram (500 grams). The whole street was a square of *Begonia fimbristipula* tea. In fact, all begonia leaves are sour, and adding some ice and sugar makes for a refreshing summer drink commonly enjoyed by locals.

Begonia fimbristipula

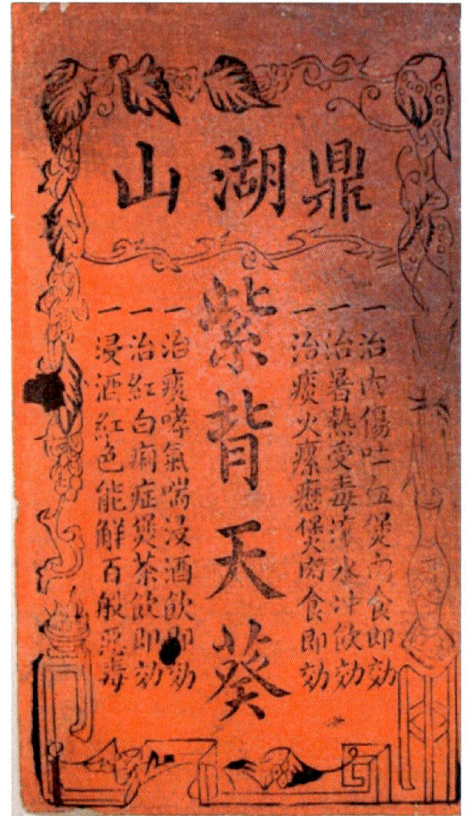

Air purification

In addition to their use in medicine and beverages, begonia leaves have a large surface that absorbs dust, releases fentanyl, and purifies the air.

Other uses: Pig feed

Once I went to Yunnan to collect *Begonia oreodoxa*. We drove for an entire day and just could not find this particular begonia variety. On the way to the hotel, I saw a farmer slowly riding a bicycle, carrying a bunch of begonia leaves behind his seat, and I quickly called to the driver to stop. "Excuse me, sir! What are you going to do with those begonia leaves?" I took a closer look and realized that these were the *Begonia oreodoxa* that we had been looking for all day. He said that it was growing all over the mountains, and he was taking it back to feed the pigs. "How do you feed this to the pigs?" I asked, and he answered, "If you cook it until it becomes soft, you can feed it to them." Apparently, *Begonia oreodoxa* leaves are rich in nutrients and can be used as animal feed.

Dr. Nakamura, a postdoctoral researcher in my lab, went to Bataan to collect begonias. The Bataan Island in the Philippines is the northernmost territory of the Philippines. The inhabitants of the island are the same as the Dawu people of Lanyu (Orchid Island). The Bataan Island pig in the lower left picture is eating *Begonia fenicis*. This picture is another proof of begonia's economic value!

Other interesting uses

Begonias are beautiful, providing artists a lot of inspiration for many creative works of art, including paintings, pottery, photography, clothing, cloth and jewelery.

After retirement, with a fund from National Taiwan University Experimental Forest, I printed a set of begonias playing cards with texts and photos, which became quite popular. Later, I created a second edition with different photos and the Chinese names.

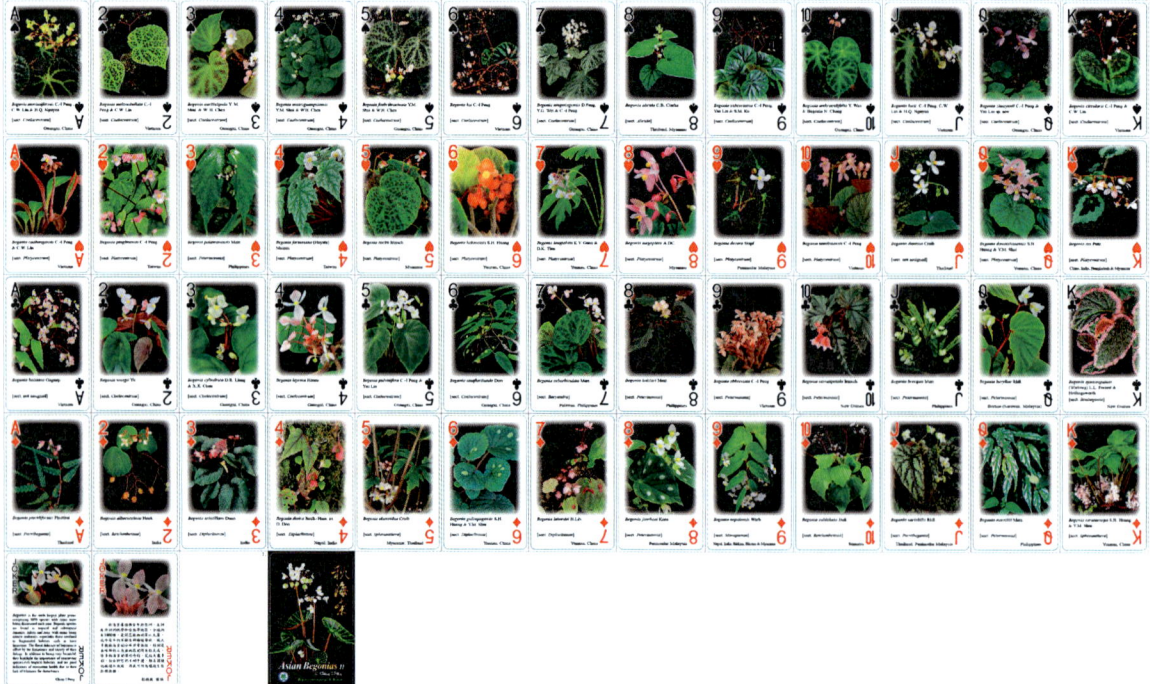

Some people are so crazy about the begonia that they will do all kinds of things for it. At the annual meeting of the American Begonia Society, everyone wears a pot of begonias on their heads on stage during the awards ceremony. Now that is something to see!

You can be even crazier than that—a Vietnamese graduate student at the Missouri Botanical Garden with a tattoo of *Begonia rex* on his shoulder.

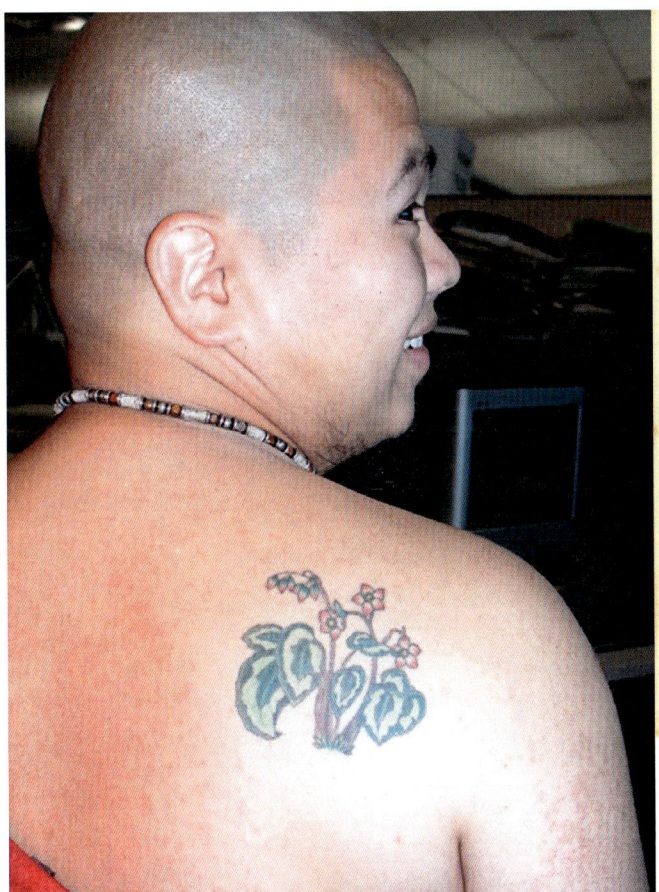

Mr. Quang Hieu Ngyuen

Begonia rex

Begonia research

Field studies are essential for—

- Field investigation and collection
- Greenhouse cultivation and observation
- Morphology classification research
- Chromosome cytology fieldwork
- Natural hybridization
- Molecular kinship analysis
- Plant geography

We can do very deep research on begonias. But the first step is always fieldwork. People with experience know that when they collect plants in the wild, they may not always get to see everything in a single trip. They may only see specimens that have not blossomed, or they may see male flowers but not female flowers, or maybe the male flowers have already wilted with the growth of fruit. It is simply impossible to expect to see begonias' every stage of life, happening all at once. Therefore, nearly all oversea collectors are willing to do anything to apply for plants to be replanted and observed carefully over time in their own country.

Field studies are essential to and extremely important in conducting proper research of the begonia. This specimen, for example, only had a few fruits when collected in the wild. We brought it back, planted it successfully and discovered that it was truly beautiful, and indeed very different from the original specimen.

Begonia ceratocarpa

And then there is identification. For example, take this dry wax leaf specimen. The first person thought it was *Begonia augustinae*, the second changed the name to *Begonia leprosa*, and a third person said it should be the *Begonia filiformisl*. Later, we made a special trip to the place of origin to find that it was a new species, and named it "*Begonia ningmingensis*".

Under close observation in the greenhouse, the sample collected and the living plant can be totally different, so we really need to collect live plants to observe and identify them properly. Once we went to the junction of Guangxi and Vietnam with the team of Dr. Yan Liu in mainland China to see this very special begonia with a pointed bump like a mountain. The same kind of begonia had different patterns on its leaves so we suspected whether this really was the Vietnamese *Begonia montaniformis*. However, the color of the flowers is different: the flowers of this begonia were white and pink, while the flowers of the *Begonia montaniformis* are yellow. The shape of the mountainous bumps were also different: the peaks of this kind were sharp, and came one after another, while the *Begonia montaniformis* peaks are distinctly heavy. Finally, we confirmed that this was a new species: *Begonia ferox*.

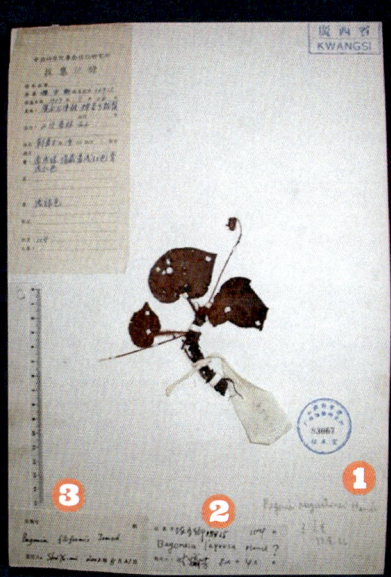

Begonia ningmingensis

Begonia ferox

Mountains in northern Vietnam

Begonia montaniformis

Begonia ferox

New species found in a floral market?

One weekend, when I was watering begonias in the greenhouse. I received a call from my student. He said excitedly," Professor! Professor! I saw a new kind of begonia in the flower market in Taichung. Should I buy it?" I doubted that a new species of Begonia could so easily be bought at a flower market —how could it be so simple? "I guarantee that this is a new species of Vietnamese begonia," he continued. I was confident in my student's knowledge of begonias, so I said to him, "Let's buy them and do some research." Then I asked him, "How many pots are there in the flower market?" "There are 6 pots. 600 dollars a pot, so that comes out to a total of 3,600 Taiwan dollars." If we really wanted to publish a new species, we would need an original type, a copy one and some group samples. "Okay! Then buy all of them!" I said. When he got back to the research facility, I saw that the begonias my student bought were amazing! So wonderful, so beautiful! Later, we went to Vietnam in hopes of collecting this variety, but unfortunately it was nowhere to be found. However, our local partner professor in Vietnam showed us a photo on his computer of the very same begonia we were looking for, and told us where he had been collecting them. After returning to Taiwan, we also confirmed with the seller of flowers that he had imported orchids from Vietnam, and shortly after planting them noticed begonia leaves growing from the roots of the orchids and they were very beautiful. Being very business-minded, he felt that this beautiful small plant could fetch a good price, so he picked it and bred it. Our team later published this new species after detailed research. We named it *Begonia kui*, after my student Shin-Ming Ku.

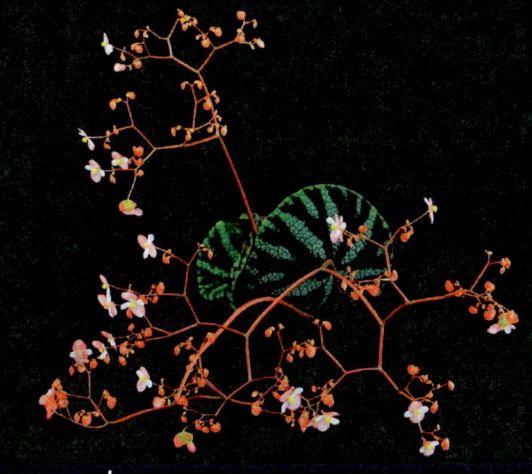

Begonia kui

Food, clothing, lodging and transportation during field collection

"While in Rome, do as the Romans do." Our food, clothing, accommodations and transportation all needed to fit with the local customs. The journey was full of thrills, excitement, and enjoyment despite several hardships, and even looking back now, it still seems like a trip that was full of fun.

Eating in the wild

When in the wild, you have to eat whatever is available. There is a dish made of sardines folded into the leaves of a begonia - a Thai-style lemon fish dish - that the locals eat. It is quite delicious!

Once when I went to Sabah, Malaysia, they arranged a camp for us. We had coffee in the morning, and everyone enjoyed it. But when I looked closely, I noticed that the color of coffee was exactly the same color as the river water... Luckily no one ended up with diarrhea from that morning!

Begonia mindorensis

I took photos of the Jino ethnic minority while I was in the Xishuangbanna. When photographing Jino people cutting vegetables, I found the action a bit familiar. Later I dug out a previous photo featuring a similar act, only this picture was of me during my first time in Xishuangbanna, preparing a specimen in the middle of the night. Whether it's the cooking of the Jino ethnic minority, or the preparation of specimens for research, we all must answer our calling!

Jino tribe, Xishuangbanna, Yunnan, China

Taiwanese Begonia botanist

Lodgings: "Full-star" accommodations

Some people ask what kind of places we stay in out in the wild, and whether they all are five-star hotels. In response I just laugh and say that we stay in "full-star" accommodations, because we sleep right under all the stars in the night sky!

And as for toilets? Once in mainland China, I happened upon double toilets. On one side sometimes there would be a man and on the other side a woman, with no wall separating them, so they could chat with each other while toileting. An impressive new type of kung fu! This is how things are out in the wild, very different from the metropolis!

And what do we do when it rains, and there is no rain gear available? The leaves of the night scented lily are very useful, and plastic bags also do just fine.

Transportation: a basketful of surprises

Field investigations take a long time, and with such a big happy family along for the ride, transportation easily became a very important consideration. Whenever our car came, we'd pile our luggage up to the roof like a mountain. Once, we even hired an ox cart without wheels to move our luggage around in the Philippines. That was very interesting.

When it came to motorcycles, seating three to a vehicle was not by any means unusual. Some of the more skilled locals could even manage up to six. However, on a stone road, even with only three to a motorcycle, a drive of an hour or two was an uncomfortable experience that I would never forget for the rest of my life!

In a tiny 3-wheeled taxi we once stuffed six people into a tiny space—thanks to some miraculous kungfu to shrink ourselves to fit!

Most of the bridges above creeks are very fragile out in the wild. You need to develop a superb sense of balance, and if you encounter a branch you can hold on to, you should thank your lucky stars.

Trekking in Search of Begonia

I started in Taiwan and then went to mainland China to collect and study begonias. I went to China at the urging of my doctoral advisor professor Dr. Peter Raven, who is the co-author and editor of the Chinese version of *Chinese Flora*, a bilingual magazine produced in collaboration with the United States. He said that the Taiwanese Begonia bio-system was doing very well, and that I might try and write about the Chinese begonia next.

At the time, I had little idea how huge a job this would turn out to be. There are about 200 species of begonias in mainland China, and I had already spent more than 10 years on 19 species in Taiwan!

Thus began our numerous to China to collect in the wild, followed by trips to many other places around the world. Global trekkings in search of begonia has enriched my life, all thanks to my enduring love for begonias.

The Philippines: A harmless surprise

Once when I went to Mindanao, Philippines, our tour guide carried a gun with him for fear of encountering rebels. This was alarming, but fortunately our guide didn't have to use it. When we returned my assistant asked, "Professor, next time you ask me to come abroad with you, will you double my insurance coverage?"

Field trips are adventures, practice gecko's adhesion kung fu and stilts can really help!

Being bitten by leech is common.

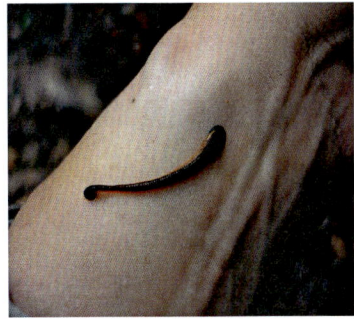
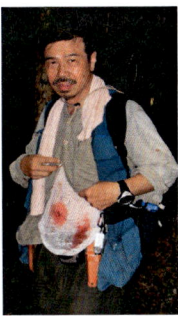

Guizhou: Beauty, snakes, and fractures

Once when I was collecting in Guizhou, just when I was taking a photo of a beauty of Miao nationality there suddenly appeared a snake behind me, and I very nearly stepped on it. That was very scary.

After dinner on the same day when I was still recovering from the shock, it started to rain, and the floor of the restaurant became slick and oily. I slipped and fell to the ground, landing flat on my back. I was sent to the hospital and the X-ray showed that my tenth rib on the left side was fractured. Until then I had no idea how painful it is to injure a rib!

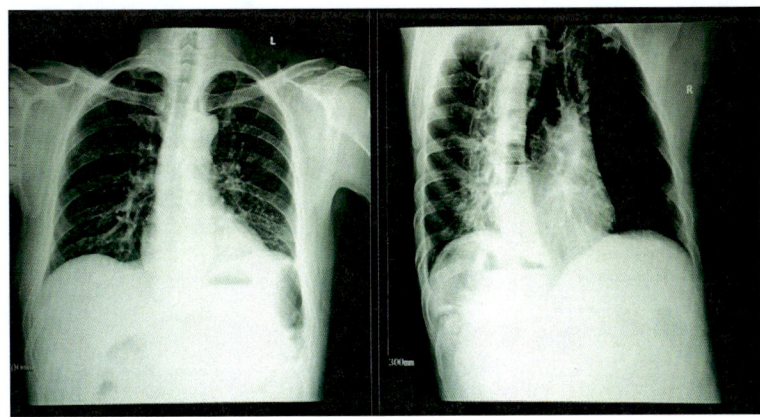

Sabah, Malaysia: Bee stings

Once I went to Sabah, Malaysia, to collect *Begonia queritziana*. When I saw the subject I was looking for I became very excited and took several pictures with my tripod. Then when I reached for the treasure, a swarm of bees flew out toward me.

I asked the guide in a panic, "What should I do?" And the guide shouted at me, "RUN!"

Then he disappeared from the slope like smoke, but I couldn't leave without the camera and tripod. When I finished packing up, I was covered by hundreds of bees already. The guide hurriedly found a national park rescuer to lift me onto a stretcher. My vision had became blurry and I vomited, feeling very nauseous the entire time. I was then lifted on stretcher to the base of the mountain to a hospital operated by a Chinese Malaysian. It turned out that the doctor's wife was a Taiwanese, so he was very happy to treat another Taiwanese for bee-stings. After an injection and medicine I was back to full health the very next day. Following the incident, I saw the *Begonia queritziana* nearly every day, but never again felt the urge to pick it!

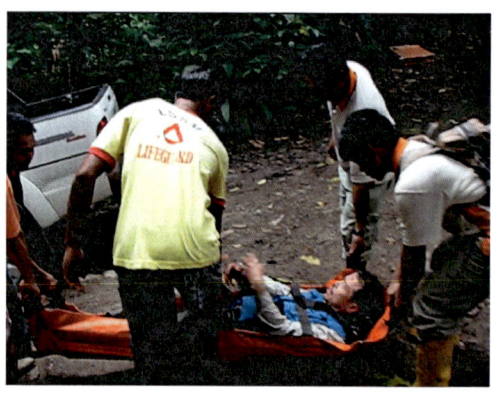

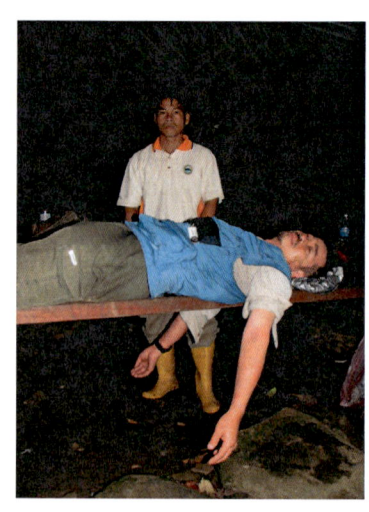

Pain experience

Whenever I see begonias flowering in the wild, I immediately have the urge to take pictures of them. Once, as I was standing on a slope setting the camera tripod up and adjusting the angle, I lost my footing and slipped. Fortunately, I hugged the trunk of the tree next to me and prevented myself from falling down the mountain. But the result wasn't entirely positive—the tree I was clinging to was a "Floss-silk tree" covered in thorns! The thorns pierced my hands all over, causing me great pain. So in the wild, anything can happen—you need to pay lots of attention, and that won't be enough!

Guangxi: Climbing up a rock wall to find new varieties

When we went to the Guangxi countryside to collect begonias, we showed locals photos and asked if they had seen the plant, and if so where. A grandmother nearby answered, "Yes! I have seen those plants nearby." So I asked her, "Can you lead the way? Can you help us find them?" and she answered, "No, I have to sell tofu in the afternoon." Later I saw the tofu, and there wasn't very much. So I just told her, "Listen, in exchange for your hard work we'll buy all of this tofu, okay?" She agreed. We walked under full sun for two hours, and our feet became very sore. Suddenly she stopped at a man-made forest and told us we'd arrived. I remarked that this was not the right environment for begonias, and that it is difficult for begonias to be seen in man-made forests.

"Look up," she said. And wow! There was a limestone mountain, straight as an arrow. The stone was very sharp and after the rain it had become even sharper and more slippery. In order to understand the ecological environment, we also had to take a photo record. We decided to climb up.

Just when we began the ascent, I heard the grandmother call out, "Grandfather don't go up, grandfather you won't make it." Turning to my assistant I asked, who is the grandfather? "That's a no brainer. It's you." came the answer. But I didn't want to lose the chance to understand the ecological environment, so I decided to climb up anyway, and ended up discovering a new species! Also accompanying us was Dr. Yan Liu from Guangxi. He said, "Professor Peng, you've worked so hard that you still insisted on climbing up, even after the grandmother warned you not to. So how about we name this new species after you?" And I thought, "Where would you ever find a cuter begonia?" and accepted this kindly suggestion with pleasure. In 2008, they published this species in my name as the *Begonia pengii*.

The Philippines: new species found

Once when I went to the Philippines to collect specimens, Professor Rosario Rubite served as our guide. She was going to participate in a seminar next day, so she had stayed at the hotel to prepare the materials. We decided that when we came back we would discuss with her the plants we had collected during the day. When I returned to the hotel in the evening, as soon as she saw the begonias that we collected she exclaimed immediately, "Wow! This is a new species! I've never seen this before!" Everyone was so excited. We quickly set to work on producing a formal description that very night: how big the flower was, how many cells in the ovary, what the cross section of the ovary was like, and so on. Everyone worked together to complete all the details. It was already ten o'clock in the evening when we finished, so I decided to break open a bag of delicious potato chips in order to celebrate the achievement! Professor Rosario said, "Professor Peng, we have worked together for so many years and have yet to publish something in your name. Shall we name this plant after you?" I replied, "No, my name has been used already for the *Begonia pengii* in Guangxi." But she wouldn't listen. "That doesn't matter," she declared triumphantly, "because this begonia can be called '*Begonia chingipengii*'". I was very happy—and humbled—to accept her kind suggestion.

Author: Ching-I Peng (彭鏡毅)
Translator: San A Lee (李山); Felicia S. Lee (李思佳)
Proof reading: Ching-Hsi Perng (彭鏡禧)
Art Editor: Amy Peng (彭敏華)
Contact info: hua0811@gmail.com

All for love: Endless Trekking in Search of Begonia by Ching-I Peng
English Translation Copyright © 2021 Amy Peng. All rights reserved.

Made in United States
North Haven, CT
17 December 2022